A NATURALIST'S GUIDE TO THE

TREES
OF
SOUTHEAST ASIA

Saw Leng Guan

JOHN BEAUFOY PUBLISHING

Penang Botanic Gardens

Reprinted in 2020

First published in the United Kingdom in 2019 by John Beaufoy Publishing Ltd
11 Blenheim Court, 316 Woodstock Road, Oxford OX2 7NS, England
www.johnbeaufoy.com

Copyright © 2019 John Beaufoy Publishing Limited
Copyright in text © 2019 Saw Leng Guan
Copyright in photographs © Saw Leng Guan, except p.15, top left © Jonathan Siau
Copyright in maps © 2019 John Beaufoy Publishing Limited

Photo Credits
Front cover: *Cassia fistula;* bottom left: *Garcinia mangostana;* bottom centre: *Elaeocarpus grandiflorus;* bottom right: *Lagerstroemia loudonii*
Back cover *Crateva religiosa*
Title page *Crescentia cujete*
Contents page *Cascabela thevetia*

All rights reserved. No part of this publication may be reproduced, stored in a retrieval system or transmitted in any form or by any means, electronic, mechanical, photocopying, recording or otherwise, without the prior written permission of the publishers.

Great care has been taken to maintain the accuracy of the information contained in this work. However, neither the publishers nor the authors can be held responsible for any consequences arising from the use of the information contained therein.

ISBN 978-1-912081-57-8

Edited by Krystyna Mayer

Designed by Gulmohur Press, New Delhi

Printed and bound in Malaysia by Times Offset (M) Sdn. Bhd.

·CONTENTS·

INTRODUCTION

This book serves as an introduction to trees and some shrubs likely to be encountered in Southeast Asia. It is by no means an exhaustive account, but it gives a flavour of the great diversity of trees found in the region. A good proportion of the species in the book are native to Southeast Asia, but common non-native species are also included. These are mainly street trees planted in rural and urban settings, or economically important trees or fruit trees. Some common secondary vegetation trees and species occurring naturally by roadsides are also included, as are some rare trees that have recently been introduced into the urban landscape. All are described in the text and illustrated with photographs. Most people find long botanical descriptions difficult to read, so these have been kept as simple as possible – and in any case, identification is often easier from the photographs than from the descriptions.

THE SPECIES DESCRIPTIONS

The species are arranged by family, then by species. Palms are easily recognizable and are included at the end of the book. For each species, the English common name is given where it is available, and common local names are used where English names do not exist. Most of the non-English names are used in Malaysia, but where possible common names from other countries are also included. Some forest plants do not have common names, and only the scientific names are given in these cases. For each species, the habit, leaves, flowers and fruits are briefly described. Concise details of the distribution and ecology of every species are also provided, followed by the plant's uses, where applicable. Under distribution, directions accompanying place names are abbreviated as follows: N (north, northern), S (south, southern), E (east, eastern), W (west, western), NE (north-east/north-eastern), SE (south-east/south-eastern) and C (central).

GEOGRAPHY, CLIMATE AND SEASONALITY

Southeast Asia is a complex geographical region comprising an archipelago of more than 25,000 islands joined to mainland Asia. The book therefore covers an area of about 4.5 million km^2, ranging from the south of China, east of continental India and west of New Guinea, to the north of Australia. Countries within this region include Myanmar, Thailand, Vietnam, Laos, Cambodia, Malaysia, Singapore, Indonesia, the Philippines, East Timor, Brunei, Christmas Island, and the Andaman and Nicobar Islands. With a population of more than 641 million people, this is one of the most populous regions in the world.

The climate of Southeast Asia is mainly tropical. It is influenced by the seasonal winds (monsoon) that bring the wet or dry season, latitude, altitude and distance from the sea. An equatorial climate develops where temperatures and rainfall are adequate for year-round plant growth, which is enjoyed in most of Peninsular Malaysia, Singapore, Borneo, Sumatra, Papua New Guinea and the mostly east-facing side of larger islands of the Philippines. In countries in continental Southeast Asia with a monsoon climate, (Thailand, Myanmar, Cambodia, Laos and Vietnam) and parts of Indonesia (mostly southern islands of eastern Java, Bali, the Sunda Islands and parts of Sulawesi) and the Philippines, the temperature is adequate year-round, but there are distinct wet and dry seasons. A strong monsoonal influence limits plant growth during drought periods, but there is sufficient rain in the wet season to sustain close canopy forest. Where rain is further limited, a tropical savannah climate develops, where close canopy forest is replaced by scattered trees, shrubs and grassland (for instance in drier parts of continental Southeast Asia, and Sumba and Timor).

A subtropical climate forms at higher latitudes, that is close to the Tropic of Cancer, for instance in northern Vietnam, northern Laos and northern Myanmar. Here temperatures during the winter months can drop to 10° C or even lower, and as a result the vegetation is very different from that in climatic zones elsewhere. The more temperate climate also enables plants from higher latitudes, for example from China and Europe, to thrive here.

Altitude further modifies temperature patterns, so mountain climates differ from lowland climates in the same region, in their lower temperatures and often less seasonal rainfall. The altitudinal range in Southeast Asia is large, ranging from a tropical lowland climate at sea level and a subtropical climate at subalpine altitude, for example on Mt Kinabalu (4,095m), in Sabah, Malaysia, to alpine and glacial conditions at higher altitudes in Puncak Jaya (4,884m), in Papua Province, Indonesia. The highest peak in Southeast Asia is Hkakabo Razi in Myanmar, at 5,881m. The mountain massifs experience climatic conditions for lowland vegetation at the bases of the mountains, climates for montane vegetation at high elevations, and an Artic climate near the peaks. Both Puncak Jaya and Hkakabo Razi reach altitudes where the conditions result in permanent snow and glaciers.

URBAN HABITATS

Increasingly, natural vegetation areas are being replaced by urban areas. Without vegetation, and with an increase in the hard surfaces of roads and buildings, urban environments in general have higher temperatures, and are drier and more polluted than other habitats. Where there are spaces available with vegetation, the soils are often compacted, poorly drained, poorly aerated, low in nutrients, and full of urban debris such as concrete, brick, glass and plastics. Such a habitat often poses a challenge to plant growth, and not many forest trees and shrubs can thrive in such difficult conditions.

TREE DIVERSITY IN SOUTHEAST ASIA

The complex geological past in the region has resulted in a very rich flora, which is estimated to contain perhaps 60,000–70,000 flowering plant species, or 15–25 per cent of the global total (Corlett, 2009). This has also translated into a very rich tree flora. In Peninsular Malaysia, for example, out of about 8,000 flowering plant species, 2,830 are trees (Saw & Chung, 2007), and Borneo is estimated to contain about 15,000 species of vascular plant, of which about 4,000 are estimated to be trees (Saw & Chung, 2007). Gardner et al. (2015)

Sandoricum koetjape

estimated that at least 2,250 tree species are native to southern Thailand, representing 75 per cent of the total tree diversity of Thailand.

With such a rich tree diversity it is not unexpected that a good number of these trees have become domesticated and were brought into cultivation. Prominent among them are fruit trees. Southeast Asia is the origin of many tropical fruit trees, including the Durian *Durio zibethinus; Rambutan, Nephelium lappaceum; Pulasan, N. ramboutan-ake;* Mango *Mangifera indica* and its relatives; *Kuni, M. odorata; Machang, M. foetida;* Longan *Dimocarpus longan;* Litchi *Litchi chinensis; Langsat, Lansium domesticum; Sentul, Sandoricum koetjape;* Mangosteen *Garcinia mangostana; Chempedak, Artocarpus integer;* Rose-apple *Syzygium aqueum;* Starfruit *Averrhoa carambola;* Pomelo *Citrus maxima* and Coconut *Cocos nucifera.* The centre of diversity of some of the genera of fruit trees is found in the region. Fruit tree species from outside the region have also become part of the local landscape, often to a point where local people view them as native species. Many come from the Americas (Cashew *Anacardium occidentale,* Custard Apple *Annona squamosa,* Soursop *A. muricata,* Cherimoya *A. cherimola,* Avocado *Persea americana,* Guava *Psidium guajava* and Chicle *Manilkara zapota*), with some from Africa (coffee *Coffea arabica* and *C. canephora*).

With urbanization of the region, numerous tree species have been introduced to provide shade and ornamental planting. Many of these native species, including a number of introductions, were initiated by forestry research institutions and often by commercial nurseries. They include *Pulai* species *Alstonia angustifolia, A. angustiloba* and *A. scholaris; Pong Pong, Cerbera manghas* and *C. odollam;* Snake Tree *Stereospermum fimbriatum; Saga, Adenanthera pavonina;* Pride of Burma *Amherstia nobilis; Cassia* species; *Mempari, Millettia pinnata; Saraca* species; Wild Cinnamon *Cinnamomum iners;* myrtles and rose-apples *Syzygium aqueum, S. borneense, S. grande, S. malaccense, S. myrtifolium* and *S. zeylanicum.* Most have been selected because they have beautiful flowers, produce spectacular blooms, provide good crown characteristics for shade, are easy to grow, can be mass propagated and can withstand harsh, often polluted urban conditions. Many of the trees have a long history in cultivation, with a mix of species that are native and exotic. The former colonial administrations established botanical gardens in Southeast Asia and also introduced many tree species into these gardens, including both economic and ornamental types. Very often

Alstonia angustiloba   *Syzygium aqueum*   *Spathodea campanulata*   *Mangifera foetida*

these species found their way into urban plantings. Some examples are the Raintree *Albizia saman*, Brown Heart *Andira inermis*, African Tulip Tree *Spathodea campanulata*, jacarandas *Jacaranda mimosifolia* and *J. obtusifolia*, Rubber Tree *Hevea brasiliensis*, *Tabebuia* species, *Brownea* species, Cashew Nut *Anacardium occidentale*, coffee (*Coffea* spp.) and Oil Palm *Elaeis guineensis*.

WHAT'S IN A NAME?

Names are important as they provide a handle to the identity of a plant. They also provide a means for us to communicate about plants, so that when we refer to a rose, for example, most of us will know what that plant is. Other than scientists, people are generally more comfortable using common or vernacular names rather than scientific names. However, this can be problematic, because very often different common names are used for the same plant species, and similar common names are also frequently applied to different species.

Vernacular names can be even more complicated – a name for a specific plant species may vary from place to place depending on the local language, and such variations are very much linked to local cultures, languages and how the plants are used. There is no regulation when it comes to common names. Often plants with little cultural or economic importance do not have common names, and in large genera or families with high species diversity, a single common name may be used for a group of species. In Peninsular Malaysia, for example, almost all species of Lauraceae are called *Medang*. The diverse tree genus *Syzygium* is all called *Kelat* in Peninsular Malaysia, but in Borneo a wide range of vernacular names is used by the many different native tribes, such as *Obah* (Dusun) in Sabah, *Ubah* (Iban and Malay), *Bah* or *Teribai* (Bidayuh), *Kelat* or *Ubar* (Kelabit), *Ubal* (Murut), *Letana* (Berawan) and *Uyah* (Kayan) in *Sarawak* (Ashton, 2011).

Scientific names are, however, regulated under an international convention. It is derived from a system, first used by the botanist, physician and zoologist Carl Linnaeus in 1753 (published in his *Species Plantarum*) to describe plant species of the world known at that time. Linnaeus introduced a two-part name system, the binomial system, consisting of a single-word genus and single-word specific epithet. This binomial system was eventually adopted by the scientific community and forms the basis of the naming of all living organisms. The naming system was adopted for plants into the Code of Botanical Nomenclature in 1867 by delegates of the First International Botanical Congress in Paris. Since then, the Code, with its regular reviews and revisions, has become the standard for naming and classification of all plant and fungal species.

This classification system is important not only in stabilizing names, but in grouping together similarly related species or taxa. For example, in *Mangifera indica*, the Common Mango, *indica* is the specific epithet for this plant, and *Mangifera* is the genus. All species of the genus *Mangifera* share similar characteristics of leaves, flowers, fruits, wood anatomy and even their biology. More recently, their genetics, that is their DNA molecular make-up, have been shown to be very similar. So, genera closely related to *Mangifera* are classified into a single family, in this case the Anacardiaceae, which also includes genera such as *Anacardium*, *Bouea*, *Campnosperma*, *Dracontomelon*, *Pentaspadon* and *Spondias*.

ACTINIDIACEAE (CHINESE GOOSEBERRIES OR KIWI FRUITS)

Saurauia fragrans

DESCRIPTION Evergreen small tree 12–20m tall. Leaves 16–28cm long, obovate or oblong. Flowers 13–17mm across, clusters in axils of leaf scars on branches, white sometimes with pink margin, heavily scented. Fruits 4cm long, globose to ovoid, whitish-green. **DISTRIBUTION AND ECOLOGY** N Sumatra and Peninsular Malaysia. Lowland to lower montane evergreen forests; also secondary forests and by roadsides, and edges of swampy forests.

Saurauia napaulensis ■ *Jelatang Gajah*

DESCRIPTION Evergreen shrub or small tree to 10m tall. Leaves 22–30cm long, brownish-green to brown beneath, obovate or oblong. Flowers 8–10mm across, clustered in axils of leaf scars on branches, pale pink, red or pinkish-white. Fruits 8–10mm long, ovoid, ripening pale green. **DISTRIBUTION AND ECOLOGY** Continental SE Asia extending from NW India through Myanmar, Thailand and Indo-China, to S China. Naturalized in Cameron Highlands, Peninsular Malaysia. Secondary growth on roadsides and forest margins in disturbed areas of montane forest, at 1,300–2,030m altitude.

Saurauia roxburghii

DESCRIPTION Evergreen shrub
or small tree 2–12m tall. Leaves
22–26cm long, elliptic to narrowly
elliptic, oblong or obovate. Flowers
8–10mm across, purple, violet or
pink, clustered in axils of leaf scars on branches. Fruits 4–11mm across, globose, ripening
white. **DISTRIBUTION AND ECOLOGY** E Nepal, India, Bangladesh, Myanmar, Indo-
China, S China, Taiwan, Japan, Thailand and Peninsular Malaysia. Lowland to montane
evergreen forests to 2,000m altitude, mainly in forest edges and secondary forests. **USES**
Fruits edible. Timber of poor quality and mainly used as firewood.

Saurauia vulcani

DESCRIPTION Evergreen shrub or small tree 5–20m tall. Leaves 25–33cm long, broadly
ovate, when young pale red. Flowers 18–20mm across, white, clustered in axils of leaf
scars on branches. Fruits 6–8mm across, globose. **DISTRIBUTION AND ECOLOGY**
Andaman Islands, Sumatra and Peninsular Malaysia. Evergreen hill to montane forests at
750–1,700m altitude; also in secondary vegetation.

Adoxaceae (Viburnums)

Viburnum sambucinum

DESCRIPTION Evergreen shrub or small tree to 10m tall. Leaves 10–25cm long, simple and opposite, elliptic. Flowers in dense, flat-topped clusters at ends of twigs, white. Fruits *c.* 0.9cm long, ripening blue-black, flattened-ovate. **DISTRIBUTION AND ECOLOGY** Sumatra, Peninsular Malaysia, Java, Borneo, Sulawesi and Lesser Sunda Islands. Frequent in moist, semi-open areas of lowland to lower montane forest.

Anacardiaceae (Cashews and Mangoes)

Anacardium occidentale ■ Cashew

(*Jagus, Gandaria, Gajus, Jambu Gajus, Jambu Bongkok*)

DESCRIPTION Evergreen tree to 12m tall, with low, spreading crown and stout, crooked trunk. Leaves 7–18cm long, obovate with blunt to rounded apex. Flowers *c.* 1.2cm across, greenish tinged pink with red stripes. Fruits *c.* 3cm long, kidney shaped, seated on swollen, fleshy yellow or red stalk (hypocarp). **DISTRIBUTION AND ECOLOGY** NE Brazil. Widely cultivated for its fruits and nuts on sandy soil near coasts; often naturalized. **USES** Fruits edible, although not much consumed. Nuts widely harvested and eaten.

Bouea macrophylla ■ Gandaria (*Kundangan, Kundang, Setar*)

DESCRIPTION Evergreen tree to 30m tall, with very dense crown and drooping lower branches. Leaves opposite, 14–30cm long, elliptic with pointed tips. Flowers *c*. 3mm across, tiny, white. Fruits 3.5–5cm long, oval or broadly ovoid, ripening yellow to orange, smooth, thin skinned, pulpy inside, edible but usually sour from wild trees. **DISTRIBUTION AND ECOLOGY** S and SE Thailand, Peninsular Malaysia, Singapore, Sumatra and W Java. Lowland forests. Sometimes cultivated in villages for its fruits. **USES** Fruits edible but rather sour even when ripe. Recently developed cultivars are sweet and have larger fruits. Young leaves sometimes eaten as a salad.

Bouea oppositifolia ■ Plum Mango (Marian Plum, *Kundang, Rumenia*)

DESCRIPTION Evergreen or briefly deciduous tree to 30m tall, with very dense crown and drooping lower branches. Leaves opposite, 4–12cm long, elliptic with pointed tips. Flowers *c*. 3mm across, tiny, white. Fruits 2.5–3.5cm long, oval or broadly ovoid, ripening yellow to orange, smooth, thin skinned, pulpy inside, edible but usually sour from wild trees. **DISTRIBUTION AND ECOLOGY** Andaman Islands, Myanmar, Thailand, Indo-China, Peninsular Malaysia, Sumatra, Banka, Billiton and Borneo. Lowland forests. Sometimes cultivated for its fruits. **USES** Fruits edible; often sour but some selected varieties are sweet.

Dracontomelon dao

■ Argus Pheasant Tree

(*Asam Kuang, Sengkuang, Sekuan*)

DESCRIPTION Deciduous tree up to 40m tall, with steep plank buttresses to 4m high. Leaves compound, clustered towards ends of twigs, each with 5–9 pairs of leaflets. Flowers white in long, hairy panicles. Fruits globose, distinctly 3-locular, *c.* 3cm across, smooth. **DISTRIBUTION AND ECOLOGY** Widely distributed from E India, to most of SE Asia and China. Lowland forests to 200m; common by streams. **USES** Fruits edible. Timber rather soft and not durable. Coloured heartwood suitable for making high-quality furniture.

Mangifera foetida ■ Horse Mango (*Machang, Bachang, Pachu*)

DESCRIPTION Medium-sized tree to 20m tall. Leaves spirally arranged, 12–28cm long. Flowers red or pink in pyramidal branched clusters. Fruits 7.5–10cm long, obliquely ovoid or oblong, slightly flattened, thick skinned, grey-green ripening yellow, flesh yellow, very fibrous, with strong, turpentine-like smell. **DISTRIBUTION AND ECOLOGY** Thailand, Peninsular Malaysia, Sumatra, Java, Borneo and Moluccas. Naturalized

in Myanmar, Lesser Sunda Islands, the Philippines and New Guinea. Lowland forests and widely cultivated. **USES** Popular fruit tree in Malaysia and Thailand. Heartwood has a streaked grain and is used for furniture. Sometimes planted as a street tree.

Mangifera indica ■ Mango (*Manga, Mempelam, Empelam*)

DESCRIPTION Evergreen or semi-deciduous tree to 30m tall, with dense, spreading crown. Leaves 12–32cm long, spirally arranged. Flowers cream or pale greenish-yellow, fragrant, in pyramidal branched clusters. Fruits 5–25cm long, oval to ovoid-oblong drupe, green ripening yellow, flesh yellow or orange, juicy, often fibrous. **DISTRIBUTION AND ECOLOGY** Widely cultivated, origin likely to be India to SE Asia. Probably native in lowland evergreen and semi-deciduous forests to lower montane forests, to 1,700m elevation. **USES** Widely cultivated for its fruits; many varieties have been selected.

Mangifera odorata ■ Fragrant Mango (Saipan Mango, *Kuini*)

DESCRIPTION Similar to M. *foetida* (see p. 13), except leaves have abrupt or shortly tapering tips and blunt to wedge-shaped flowers. Flowers white ageing to pink, in clusters, with yellow-green main stalk and pinkish branches. Fruits obliquely ovoid-ellipsoid or oblong with flat, fibrous seeds, sweetly fragrant, without turpentine-like smell. **DISTRIBUTION AND ECOLOGY** Widely cultivated in SE Asia. Not known in the wild; a hybrid between M. *foetida* and M. *indica*. **USES** Fruits edible and often sold in village markets.

Pentaspadon curtisii ■ Curtis's Pelong

DESCRIPTION Deciduous tree to 30m tall, with graceful feathery crown and slender buttressed trunk. Leaves compound, *c.* 30cm long, clustered near ends of twigs, 3–5 pairs of leaflets with terminal leaflet. Flowers tiny, white, in terminal clusters. Fruits 2–2.5cm long, ellipsoid, yellow-green ripening brown with pale dots and 1 large seed. **DISTRIBUTION AND ECOLOGY** Endemic in S Thailand and NW Peninsular Malaysia (including Langkawi). Semi-deciduous lowland forests on limestone hills. **USES** Timber moderately durable. Fruits edible after boiling.

Spondias dulcis
■ Great Hog Plum (Golden Apple, Otaheite Apple, Yellow Plum, Ambrarella, *Kedondong*)

DESCRIPTION Small evergreen or deciduous tree 6–20m tall. Leaves compound, 20–60cm long, 9–25 leaflets with terminal leaflet. Flowers small, white, inconspicuous in terminal clusters. Fruits 6–9cm long, ovoid, green turning golden-yellow when ripe. **DISTRIBUTION AND ECOLOGY** Only known from cultivation, probably arose in tropical Asia. **USES** Fruits are edible, eaten raw or cooked. When green, the fruit is crisp and slightly acidic. Young leaves are also edible as salad or cooked.

ANNONACEAE (CUSTARD APPLES OR SOURSOPS)

Annona muricata ■ Soursop (*Buah Belanda*)

DESCRIPTION Small evergreen tree 3–10m tall. Leaves 8–16cm long, oblong-obovate. Flowers *c*. 3cm long on main trunk and branches, pale green, solitary. Fruits 15–25cm long,

irregularly ellipsoid or ovoid, covered with soft prickles, dark green when ripe. **DISTRIBUTION AND ECOLOGY** Caribbean and C America.

Coastal limestone and lowland woodland. **USES** Widely cultivated throughout the tropics for its edible fruits. One of the first fruits carried from the Americas to the Old World tropics. Fruits eaten raw, and also often juiced. Leaves known to have medicinal properties.

Cananga odorata ■ Cananga (*Kenanga, Ilang-ilang, Ylang Ylang, Nyai*)

DESCRIPTION Evergreen tree to 30m tall, with irregular crown that has stiff, spreading branches. Leaves 8–20cm long, often drooping, oblong to narrowly ovate with tapering tips. Flowers up to 8cm long, pale green turning to yellow, very fragrant at flower maturity,

in short, unbranched clusters. Fruits 1.5–2.5cm long, on individual stalks, arranged in dense cluster of stalked fruits, dark green ripening blackish. **DISTRIBUTION AND ECOLOGY** Widely distributed from India throughout SE Asia to N Australia. Common in lowland forests. Often cultivated for its fragrant flowers. **USES** Oil from flowers is extracted for perfumes.

Monoon longifolium ■ Indian Mast Tree (False Asoka, Mast Tree, Weeping Mast Tree)

DESCRIPTION Evergreen tree to 18m tall, with straight trunk, the wild form with a thick, bushy crown. Commonly cultivated form 'Pendula' has a dense, narrowly columnar crown and slender, drooping twigs. Leaves 12–23cm long, narrowly lanceolate, with tapering tips and wavy margins. Flowers 1.2–2cm long, pale green to cream or yellowish, not fragrant, in dense groups at leaf axils. Fruitlets 1.5–2cm on stout individual stalk; numerous fruitlets, with up to 15 on common woody stalk, ovoid, ripening yellow to black. **DISTRIBUTION AND ECOLOGY** India and Sri Lanka. Lowland forests. **USES** Widely planted as an ornamental (especially 'Pendula' form).

Polyalthia stenopetala

DESCRIPTION Small evergreen tree to 10m tall.
Leaves 14–18cm long, young leaves reddish, turning
to pale yellow before
turning green. Flowers
pink to red, in dense
groups on woody knobs
along trunk and main
branches. Fruits 2–3cm
long on slender stalk,
oval to oblong, ripening
red. **DISTRIBUTION
AND ECOLOGY**
S Thailand and
Peninsular Malaysia.
Lowland evergreen
forests.

APOCYNACEAE (DOGBANES)

Alstonia angustifolia ■ Red-leafed Pulai (Hard Alstonia, *Pulai Peninpu Paya*)

DESCRIPTION Tree to 50m tall, diameter to 70cm,
base fluted or with buttresses. Leaves in whorls of
3 (rarely 4), obovate. Flowers in dense clusters,
fragrant, corolla pale yellow, rusty pubescent
outside. Fruits in paired follicles. **DISTRIBUTION
AND ECOLOGY** Sumatra, Peninsular Malaysia,
Singapore and Borneo. Lowland to hill dipterocarp
forests to 800m altitude; often in seasonally
swampy forests, sometimes in peat forests. **USES**
Timber similarly used to that of *A. angustiloba* (see
opposite); sometimes used in landscaping.

Alstonia angustiloba

■ Common Pulai (*Pulai*)

DESCRIPTION Tree to 50m tall, diameter to 1m; characteristic high, fluted bole with pagoda-shaped crown. Leaves arranged in whorls of 4–7(–9). Creamy-white to pale yellow, fragrant flowers arranged in dense clusters. Fruits in paired pendulous follicles. Trees often flower synchronously, when the whole crown is covered in creamy-white to pale yellow flowers. **DISTRIBUTION AND ECOLOGY** Thailand, Sumatra, Peninsular Malaysia, Singapore, Borneo and Java. Native in lowland forests to 1,000m elevation, and often in secondary forests. **USES** Timber is not durable and is used as a light hardwood, traded under Pulai. Tree has an attractive pagoda crown and is widely used in landscaping.

Alstonia macrophylla ■ Broad-leafed Pulai (False Pulai, *Pulai Penipu Bukit*)

DESCRIPTION Evergreen tree to 50m tall, diameter to 100cm, buttresses usually absent or low and only shallowly spreading. Leaves in whorls of 3–4. Cream to white flowers arranged in terminal, rather lax inflorescence. Flowers small, *c.* 7mm long. Fruits in paired pendulous follicles. **DISTRIBUTION AND ECOLOGY** Widely distributed in continental India, SE Asia and S China. Common in lowland and hill forests to 1,000m altitude, and in secondary forests. **USES** Timber traded with that of *A. angustiloba* (see above) as Pulai. Timber hard and used to make furniture and flooring.

Alstonia scholaris ■ Indian Pulai

DESCRIPTION
Evergreen or briefly deciduous tree to 50–60m tall, diameter more than 130cm, with pagoda-shaped crown, quite similar to that of *A. angustiloba* (see p. 19). Leaves arranged in whorls of 4–8, glaucous below. Inflorescences in dense clusters,

often quite crowded, flowers fragrant, creamy-white to pale yellow. Fruits in paired pendulous follicles. Trees often flower synchronously, when the whole crown is covered with flowers. **DISTRIBUTION AND ECOLOGY** Widespread species ranging from Indian subcontinent to S China, SE Asia and N Australia. Native in lowland forests to 1,000m elevation, and sometimes in secondary forests. **USES** Timber not durable and used as light hardwood. It was used for slates in schools (hence its species epithet name, *scholaris*). Tree has an attractive pagoda crown and is widely used in landscaping.

Alstonia spatulata ■ Marsh Pulai (*Pulai Paya, Basong*)

DESCRIPTION Similar to *A. angustiloba* (see p. 19) in habit but shorter in height, to 25m, sometimes forming plank buttresses to 1.2m high. Leaves in whorls of 3–4(–5), without distinct intrapetiolar stipule at base of petiole. Inflorescence 3–11cm long, rather lax, few flowered; flowers cream-white to yellow. Fruits a pair of follicles, 12–25cm long. **DISTRIBUTION AND ECOLOGY** Widespread throughout SE Asia. Common in lowland forests, frequently in swampy environments in freshwater swamp and peat-swamp forests. Also grows on margins of abandoned tin-mining ponds; here it sometimes grows floating on sedge/grass mats. **USES** Timber is used for carving. Root wood is one of the lightest woods in the world and is used as a substitute for cork.

Calotropis gigantea ■ Giant Indian Milkweed (Crown Flower, Ivory Plant, *Kemengu*)

DESCRIPTION Evergreen bushy shrub to 4m tall. Leaves large, thick, covered with pale silvery-green wax and woolly hairs on both sides. Inflorescence in racemes towards apex, with clusters of large white to lilac flowers. Fruits a pair of fat, kidney-shaped, fleshy follicles, ripening and splitting apart to reveal wind-dispersed light seeds attached with woolly hairs. **DISTRIBUTION AND ECOLOGY** Native in drier climates of S India to S China, Indo-China and Indonesia. In Malaysia it has naturalized in coastal areas. **USES** Sometimes grown as an ornamental.

Cascabela thevetia ■ Yellow Oleander (Trumpet Flower, Lucky Nut)

DESCRIPTION Shrub to small evergreen tree to 10m tall. Leaves linear, spirally arranged. Flowers in axils of branches, large, 6–7cm long, trumpet shaped, yellow to creamy-pink. Fruits globular with longitudinal ridge across, green ripening black, 3–4.5cm across. **DISTRIBUTION AND ECOLOGY** Mexico, where it grows in evergreen lowland or riparian forests; naturalized throughout tropical C and S America. **USES** All parts of the plant are poisonous. Widely grown as an ornamental for its attractive leaves and flowers.

Cerbera manghas ■ Pink-Eyed Cerbera (*Pong Pong, Buta Buta*)

DESCRIPTION Very similar to C. *odollam* (see below), except for its smaller leaves and flowers with pink eyes. Fruits oblong or ellipsoid, *c.* 5–12cm long. **DISTRIBUTION AND ECOLOGY** Widespread from the Seychelles through E Asia and throughout SE Asia to the Pacific islands and N Australia. Common on sandy and rocky seashores, and sandy coastal heaths. **USES** Commonly planted as a street tree. Timber used for charcoal. Seeds can be made into a fish poison, and oil extracted from the seeds is made into candles. Seeds are extremely poisonous.

Cerbera odollam ■ Yellow-eyed Cerbera (*Pong Pong, Buta Buta*)

DESCRIPTION Small evergreen tree or bush to 12m tall, diameter to 20cm. Leaves spirally arranged. Inflorescence in terminal panicles, few to many flowered. Flowers white, corolla white with yellow eye, *c.* 1.5–2.5cm long. Fruits spherical to ovoid, green when

mature, *c.* 5–8cm long. Fruits buoyant, and dispersed by water. **DISTRIBUTION AND ECOLOGY** Widely distributed from Sri Lanka and S India to coastal regions of SE Asia to W Pacific islands. Mostly coastal on tidal mud or sand or in mangrove swamps. **USES** Has poisonous sap and can cause blindness. Seeds are also very poisonous. Often planted as a street tree.

Dyera costulata ■ *Jelutong*

DESCRIPTION Emergent deciduous tree to 80m tall, diameter to 3m. Leaves in whorls of 4–8. Inflorescence 4–18cm long, many flowered with cream corolla, flowers 3–5mm long. Fruits in paired divergent follicles, woody, dehiscing at maturity, 18–40cm long. Deciduous, and flowers for about 10 days on bare branches immediately after leaves are shed. Light winged seeds dispersed by wind. **DISTRIBUTION AND ECOLOGY** S Thailand, Sumatra, Peninsular Malaysia and Borneo. Lowland forests to 500m altitude; occasionally on ridges in swampy forests. **USES** Key timber tree; commercially important in manufacture of pencils.

Holarrhena pubescens ■
Jasmine Tree (Bitter Oleander, Easter Tree)

DESCRIPTION Evergreen shrub to small tree to 15m tall. Leaves opposite. Flowers in clusters of white flowers, 1–2cm long, very fragrant. Fruits in paired follicles, pendulous, 18–43cm long. **DISTRIBUTION AND ECOLOGY** Native in subcontinental India to Indo-China and S China. Understorey plant in deciduous forests. **USES** Often cultivated as an ornamental and also known as a medicinal plant.

Kibatalia maingayi

DESCRIPTION Evergreen tree to 40m tall, diameter to 120cm. Leaves opposite, 5–14cm long. Flowers in lax terminal clusters, white to pale creamy-yellow, 2–2.5cm across. Fruits in paired follicles, slender, 8–50cm long. **DISTRIBUTION AND ECOLOGY** Thailand, Sumatra, Peninsular Malaysia, Borneo and the Philippines. Common in lowland to hill forests.

Kopsia arborea ■ Penang Sloe (Shrub Vinca)

DESCRIPTION Evergreen tree to 14m tall, diameter to 30cm. Leaves opposite, dying red. Flowers clustered in terminal inflorescence, white, 2–4cm long. Fruits with only 1 carpel developing into oblique ellipsoid or subglobose drupe, ripening blue-black. **DISTRIBUTION AND ECOLOGY** Widely distributed in Andaman and Nicobar Islands, S China, SE Asia and Australia (Queensland). Lowland evergreen forests. **USES** Cultivated as a street tree, particularly in Penang. A large, mature one grows in the Penang Botanic Gardens, and its seeds are the source of the street trees found in Penang. Otherwise very rare, and considered Critically Endangered in Malaysia.

Kopsia fruticosa ■ Pink Kopsia (Shrub Vinca)

DESCRIPTION Evergreen woody shrub or occasionally small tree to 5m tall. Leaves opposite. Flowers in terminal clusters, pink fading to white with dark red throat, 3–5cm long. Fruits fleshy drupes, 2.5cm long. **DISTRIBUTION AND ECOLOGY** Myanmar. Lowland forests. **USES** Cultivated for its attractive flowers.

Kopsia singapurensis ■ Singapore Kopsia

DESCRIPTION Evergreen tree to 12m tall, diameter to 24cm. Leaves opposite. Flowers in loose terminal clusters, corolla white with red eye. Fruits oblique ellipsoid, 2.5–5mm long. **DISTRIBUTION AND ECOLOGY** Endemic in Peninsular Malaysia and Singapore. Lowland dipterocarp forests on riverbanks, or swampy forests to 200m altitude. **USES** Sometimes planted as an ornamental, but not as popular as *K. fruticosa* (see above).

Plumeria obtusa
▪ Great White Frangipani
(Frangipani, *Kemboja, Bunga Kubur*)

DESCRIPTION Small deciduous or evergreen tree to more than 12m tall, with low, rounded crown. Spirally arranged leaves *c*. 15–25cm long with blunt tips. Inflorescences in large terminal clusters of white flowers. Flowers white, strongly fragrant, 9–10cm across. Fruits in twin, cylindrical, recurved pods, *c*. 15–17.5cm long. **DISTRIBUTION AND ECOLOGY** Native in tropical Americas, where it grows coastal forests. **USES** Widely cultivated and very popular ornamental tree. In Malaysia often planted in Malay cemeteries (*Bunga Kubur* means Grave Flower).

Plumeria rubra ▪ Nosegay Frangipani (Frangipani, Red Frangipani, *Kemboja*)

DESCRIPTION Large deciduous or evergreen shrub or small tree to 8–10m tall. Leaves spirally arranged, 30–50cm long, with pointed tips. Flowers on terminal clusters, often flowering profusely with different ranges of colour, from common pink to white with shades of yellow in the centre, to burgundy red. Fruits in twin, cylindrical, recurved pods, *c*. 17.5cm long. **DISTRIBUTION AND ECOLOGY** Native in tropical Americas in dry, hot, rocky habitats of forests and mountain slopes, and on brushy savannah. **USES** Widely cultivated and very popular as an ornamental tree.

Tabernaemontana corymbosa

■ Great Rosebay (Flower of Love, *Jelutong Badak*)

DESCRIPTION Evergreen tree to 12m tall, diameter to 20cm. Leaves opposite. Flowers in clusters of up to 25 or more, white with yellow throats, 2–3cm long. Fruits in paired, fleshy, orange, globose to obliquely ellipsoid follicles, 5–7cm long. Fruits dehiscing to expose seeds with red or orange aril. **DISTRIBUTION AND ECOLOGY** Widespread in SE Asia and S China. Frequent in lowland and hill forests to 1,000m altitude. **USES** Occasionally planted as an ornamental.

Tabernaemontana divaricata ■ East Indian Rosebay

(Pinwheel Flower, Ceylon Jasmine, *Susun Kelapa*)

DESCRIPTION Evergreen shrub or small tree to 5m tall, with open, spreading crown. Leaves opposite. Flowers in terminal clusters of up to 25, white with yellow throat, often fragrant, 2–3.5cm long. Fruits in paired follicle, oblique-ellipsoid with pointed tips, ripening orange. **DISTRIBUTION AND ECOLOGY** Native in N India, Myanmar and Thailand. Lowland forests. **USES** Often cultivated for its white flowers. Many Hindu families have this shrub, and its flowers are used for prayer.

Tabernaemontana polyneura

DESCRIPTION
Evergreen tree
to 21m tall.
Leaves opposite,
3.2–25cm long.
Flowers in sparse
clusters, white
petals with yellow
corolla tube and
eye, 1.5–2cm long.
Fruits oblique-
ellipsoid, to 37cm
long. **DISTRIBUTION AND ECOLOGY** Endemic
in Peninsular Malaysia. Rare tree of hill and lower
montane forests.

Wrightia antidysenterica ■ Snow Flake
(Star of Milky Way, Sri Lanka Wrightia)

DESCRIPTION Slender evergreen shrub
to 3m tall. Leaves opposite, 3–10cm long.
Flowers in sparsely branched clusters, pure
white, 1.7–2.8cm long. Fruits in paired
follicles, 20–38cm long. **DISTRIBUTION
AND ECOLOGY** Sri Lanka. Ecology
unknown. **USES** Widely cultivated as an
ornamental shrub in Thailand and Malaysia.
Rarely fruits in Thailand and Malaysia.
Plants often propagated by marcotting and
through stem cuttings.

Wrightia religiosa ■ Water Jasmine (Common Wrightia)

DESCRIPTION Evergreen shrub or small tree to 5m tall. Leaves opposite, 1.5–8.2cm long. Flowers in branched terminal clusters, white, pendulous, fragrant, 1–2.5cm long. Fruits in paired follicles, 8.5–17.5cm long, linear. **DISTRIBUTION AND ECOLOGY** Native in Thailand, Cambodia and Peninsular Malaysia. Scattered in lowland forests and roadsides, and probably an escape from cultivation. **USES** Very popular as an ornamental shrub. Commonly used as a bonsai species.

BIGNONIACEAE (BIGNONIAS)

Crescentia cujete ■ Calabash Tree

DESCRIPTION Small evergreen or deciduous tree 6–9m tall, with low, multiple branches. Leaves to c. 25cm long, obovate, arranged in clusters on branches. Flowers 5–6.5cm long, borne singly on stout stalks on trunk and branches, light green, bell shaped. Fruits large, globose to ovoid, 10–30cm diameter, green ripening brown with very hard rind. **DISTRIBUTION AND ECOLOGY** Widely cultivated in C and S America; wild origin uncertain. **USES** Widely grown as an ornamental in the tropics. Fruits used to make bowls, cups, jugs, water containers and other utensils, as well as decorated ornaments and musical instruments.

Handroanthus chrysanthus ■ Golden Trumpet Tree (Golden Goddess)

DESCRIPTION Deciduous tree to 24m tall. Leaves opposite, palmately compound with 5 leaflets, *c.* 25cm across. Flowers *c.*

5cm long, large, showy, tubular, yellow, in compact terminal clusters; whole crown often blooms after leaf fall. Fruits slender, flattened capsules, *c.* 25cm long. **DISTRIBUTION AND ECOLOGY** Sometimes naturalized in SE Asia. In C and N S America, found in deciduous tropical forests. **USES** Often planted as an ornamental for its spectacular yellow blooms.

Jacaranda mimosifolia
■ Blue Jacaranda (Jacaranda, Black Poui, Fern Tree)

DESCRIPTION Small deciduous tree 10–20m tall.
Leaves bipinnately compound, opposite, to 45cm
long with fine leaflets (fern-like). Flowers to 5cm
long, bell-shaped in clusters to 30cm long, purple.
Fruit a woody seed pod, rounded, flattened, *c.*
5cm across with winged seeds. **DISTRIBUTION
AND ECOLOGY** Bolivia and Argentina. Bushland,
grassland, wooded ravines and riverbanks. **USES**
Often grown as an ornamental. Does best in

climates with strong
seasonality, where it
produces complete
purple blooms. In
wetter areas lacking
seasonality, remains
evergreen with poor
flowering.

Jacaranda obtusifolia ■ Fernleaf Jacaranda (Jacaranda, Green Ebony)

DESCRIPTION Small semi-deciduous to fully
deciduous tree 4–15m tall, with loosely formed
crown. Similar to *J. mimosifolia* (see
above), except leaflets are blunt tipped and
flowers are paler with shallower cups. Fruit a
woody seed pod, rounded, flattened, *c.* 5cm
across, with winged seeds. **DISTRIBUTION
AND ECOLOGY** Highland forests of N and
C S America, from Venezuela to Bolivia.
USES Often grown as an ornamental. Like *J.
mimosifolia*, does best in climates with strong
seasonality, where it produces better flowering.

Kigelia africana ■ Sausage Tree

DESCRIPTION Deciduous or semi-deciduous tree to 10m tall. Leaves opposite, or in whorls of three, pinnately compound, 9–20cm long, crowded near ends of branches, leaflets 3–5 pairs with terminal leaflet, ovate-oblong to elliptic-ovate. Flowers large, dark maroon with yellow veining, in pendulous sprays of up to 12 flowers. Fruits large, sausage shaped, to 60cm long and weighing to 7kg. **DISTRIBUTION AND ECOLOGY** Native in tropical plains of Africa. **USES** Sometimes cultivated as an ornamental. Fresh fruits poisonous, but after drying, roasting or fermentation they can be eaten.

Millingtonia hortensis ■ Indian Cork-tree (Cork Tree)

DESCRIPTION Deciduous or semi-evergreen tree to 15m tall. Bark deeply irregularly cracked, thick and corky. Leaves opposite, 40–100cm long, 2 or 3 times pinnate. Flowers 9–11cm long, white, in spreading branched clusters, strongly fragrant. Fruits 30–40cm long, straight, flattened capsule, splitting lengthways and exposing winged seeds. **DISTRIBUTION AND ECOLOGY** S Myanmar, Thailand and Indo-China. Open deciduous forests. **USES** Often planted as an ornamental.

Oroxylum indicum
■ Midnight Horror (Broken Bones Plant)

DESCRIPTION Evergreen or semi-evergreen tree to 15m tall, often much branched from the base in older trees with irregular sparsely branched crown. Leaves compound, opposite, very large, *c.* 150cm long, 3-4 x pinnate. Flowers 8–12cm long, very large, dirty yellow to pink-violet in upright clusters held above the crown, opening at night, dropping off by daybreak. Fruits 30–120cm long, sword-shaped. **DISTRIBUTION AND ECOLOGY** Widespread in India, Sri Lanka, Nepal, Myanmar, Thailand, S China, Vietnam, Peninsular Malaysia, Sumatra, Java, Timor, Borneo, Sulawesi and the Philippines. Forest gaps and secondary growth areas. The flowers are bat pollinated. **USES** Young fruits are edible. Wood used for matchsticks, paper pulp and firewood.

Parmentiera cereifera ■ Candle Tree

DESCRIPTION Small tree to 7m tall, with bushy habit. Leaves opposite, trifoliate. Flowers solitary or borne in cluster of up to 4, greenish-white. Fruit a tubular-shaped berry to 60cm long, green ripening yellow, waxy in texture. **DISTRIBUTION AND ECOLOGY** Atlantic coast of Panama. Limestone woodland. **USES** Sometimes grown as an ornamental. Fruits edible. Occasionally planted as an ornamental.

Radermachera pinnata subsp. *acuminata*
■ Lowland Fox-glove Tree

DESCRIPTION Evergreen tree to 20m tall, with narrow crown. Leaves bipinnately compound, opposite, 20–45cm long. Flowers c. 3cm long, cream with yellow-orange and pink markings, in branched terminal clusters. Fruits 15–35cm long, narrowly cylindrical, flattened capsule, twisting and hanging in loose clusters. **DISTRIBUTION AND ECOLOGY** S Thailand, Peninsular Malaysia, Borneo, Sumatra and the SW Philippines. Scattered in freshwater swamps or along streams; also recorded on limestone hills. **USES** Occasionally planted as an ornamental.

Spathodea campanulata
■ African Tulip Tree

DESCRIPTION Evergreen or semi-deciduous tree to 35m tall, with dense, bushy, oval crown. Leaves to 50cm long, opposite, pinnately compound. Flowers large, to 10cm long, bell shaped, orange to red. Fruit a capsule, 15–23cm long, flattened. **DISTRIBUTION AND ECOLOGY** Native in tropical forests of sub-Saharan Africa. Naturalized in Peninsular Malaysia and Singapore. **USES** Widely cultivated as an ornamental in the tropics. Yellow variety occasionally grown. Timber used for plywood.

Tabebuia aurea ▪ Silver Trumpet Tree
(Tree of Gold, Paraguayan Silver Trumpet Tree)

DESCRIPTION Small deciduous tree to 8m tall, with bushy crown. Leaves opposite, palmately compound, with 5–7 leaflets, each leaflet 6–18cm long, covered with silvery scales on both surfaces. Flowers tubular, *c*. 6.5cm diameter, bright yellow in loose clusters. Fruits slender, flattened capsules, *c*. 10cm long. **DISTRIBUTION AND ECOLOGY** Suriname, Brazil, E Bolivia, Peru, Paraguay and N Argentina. Riparian areas and dry deciduous forests. **USES** Planted as an ornamental. Does best in areas with drier climates, where the tree blossoms with yellow flowers after shedding its leaves.

Tabebuia rosea ▪ Rosy Trumpet Tree (Pink Poui, Pink Tecoma)

DESCRIPTION Deciduous tree to 30m tall, with irregular crown. Leaves opposite, palmately compound, with 5 leaflets. Flowers 5–10cm long, large, showy, tubular, in various shades of pink to purple and white in loose clusters. Fruits slender, flattened capsules, *c*. 35cm long. **DISTRIBUTION AND ECOLOGY** S Mexico to Venezuela and Ecuador. Lowland deciduous forests to 1,200m elevation. **USES** Widely planted as an ornamental and street tree. In climates with distinct dry seasons, the leaves typically drop at the beginning of the dry season, and subsequent dry conditions trigger a mass blooming near the end of the dry season. In ever-wet climates, flowers tend to boom intermittently throughout the year.

Bonnetiaceae

Ploiarium alternifolium
■ Cicada Tree (*Riang Riang, Sesudu Paya*)

DESCRIPTION Evergreen shrub or small tree to 15m tall, with narrow crown. Leaves 9–15cm long, spirally arranged. Flowers *c.* 3cm across, petals free, white flushed pink, solitary at upper leaf axils or several flowers close together near ends of twigs. Fruits narrowly ovoid capsules, *c.* 2cm long. **DISTRIBUTION AND ECOLOGY** Thailand, Cambodia, Peninsular Malaysia, Singapore, Sumatra, Riau, Lingga and Borneo. In secondary growth, heath vegetation, open swampy areas, and sometimes along exposed mountain tops or rocky coasts.

Boraginaceae (Borage)

Cordia sebestena ■ Scarlet Cordia (Geiger Tree, Siricote)

DESCRIPTION Shrubby tree to 10m with dense bushy rounded crown. Leaves *c.* 20cm long, ovate with wavy margins. Flowers *c.* 5cm across, tubular and flaring, dark orange, in terminal dense clusters. Fruits *c.* 5cm long, pear-shaped. **DISTRIBUTION AND ECOLOGY** Native to the American tropics, S Florida (USA), the Bahamas, southwards throughout C America. Seashore, mangrove fringe and open habitats. **USES** Widely grown as an ornamental.

CALOPHYLLACEAE (IRONWOODS)

Calophyllum inophyllum ■ Alexandrian Laurel
(*Penaga Laut*)

DESCRIPTION Medium-sized tree to 20m tall, with spreading crown. Leaves 8–18cm long, opposite, broadly elliptic-oblong. Flowers 2–2.5cm long, white, in loose clusters. Fruits *c.* 3cm across, globose to ovoid, smooth, dull green to brownish when ripe. **DISTRIBUTION AND ECOLOGY** Very widespread species from E Africa, Madagascar, Indian Ocean islands, Sri Lanka, India, SE Asia, Taiwan and SE China (Hainan), to N Australia, New Caledonia and Pacific islands. Common along

beaches and rocky coasts. **USES** Widely planted as an ornamental street tree. Timber rich red-brown with fine grain, and fairly durable. Fruits sold as punnai nuts, and yield a dark green oil that is strongly aromatic but mildly toxic.

Mesua ferrea ■ Ceylon Ironwood (*Penaga Lilin*)

DESCRIPTION Evergreen tree to 24m tall, with very dense, narrowly conical crown and slender, drooping branches. Leaves 5–13cm long, opposite, narrowly elliptic, pale or white (glaucous) on under surface. Flowers large and showy, 5–8cm across, white, very fragrant, solitary or in pairs at leaf axils. Fruits 2.8–3.5cm long, ovoid to ellipsoid, seated on persistent woody sepals at base. **DISTRIBUTION AND ECOLOGY** Sri Lanka, SW India, Andaman Islands, Myanmar, Thailand, Vietnam and Peninsular Malaysia. Lowland evergreen forests to 500m. **USES** Extremely hard and durable; red-brown timber is traded as Ceylon Ironwood. Also widely planted as an ornamental street tree.

CAPPARACEAE (CAPERS)

Crateva adansonii ■ Caper Tree
(Garlic Pear Tree, India Dalur)

DESCRIPTION Small deciduous tree to 20m tall. Leaves trifoliate, leaflets 7.5–12cm long with distinct short stalk, broadly ovate. Flowers *c.* 5cm across, in loose terminal clusters, pale green turning white at anthesis fading into pale yellow, appearing before or just after flush of new leaves. Fruits 3–5cm diameter, globose, yellowish.

DISTRIBUTION AND ECOLOGY India, Sri Lanka, Myanmar, S China, Indo-China and Thailand. In streams and on riverbanks. **USES** Planted as an ornamental. Used in Ayurvedic medicine in India. Young shoots and flowers are edible.

Crateva religiosa ■ Sacred Garlic Pear (Spider Tree, Temple Tree, *Dalur*)

DESCRIPTION Small deciduous tree 6–15m tall. Leaves trifoliate, leaflets 8–16cm long, stalkless or nearly so. Flowers 3–6cm across, in loose terminal clusters, greenish-white turning yellowish after opening, appearing before or just after flush of new leaves. Fruits 3–5cm diameter, subglobose to ovoid, yellowish. **DISTRIBUTION AND ECOLOGY** India, most of SE Asia, Solomon Islands, Micronesia and Polynesia. Swampy habitats. **USES** Fruits edible. Often grown in temples and sometimes as an ornamental.

CASUARINACEAE (SHE-OAKS AND CASUARINAS)

Casuarina equisetifolia ■ Casuarina (*Rhu*)

DESCRIPTION Evergreen tree to 30m tall, with narrowly conical crown when young, becoming irregular and untidy with ascending main branches. Leaves reduced to tiny scales arranged in whorls of 7–8 teeth at intervals of *c.* 1cm along pendulous, flexible green twigs, resembling pine needles. Flowers minute, unisexual, with male and female flowers in different clusters. Male flowers in simple spikes; female flowers in dense globular heads. Fruits in cone-like heads, *c.* 0.5cm diameter. Seeds winged.

DISTRIBUTION AND ECOLOGY S Thailand, throughout Malaysia, Indonesia, the Philippines, N and E Australia, Melanesia and Polynesia. Common along coastal beaches. **USES** Often grown as a street tree. Timber very hard and difficult to work with; it makes excellent firewood and charcoal.

Gymnostoma nobile ■ Rhu Ronang

DESCRIPTION Evergreen tree to 40m tall; crown conical when young, becoming roundish. Needle-shaped twigs with few lateral branches, mostly exceeding 10cm long. Leaves scale-like in whorls of 4 at intervals of 0.5–1cm. Flowers minute, unisexual, with male and female flowers in different clusters. Male flowers in simple terminal spikes; female flowers in terminal heads. Fruits in cone-like heads, globose, *c.* 2.2cm across. **DISTRIBUTION AND ECOLOGY** Palawan Islands and Borneo. Lowland and hill heath forests to 1,000m, on sandstone and ultramafic rocks. **USES** As an ornamental in streets and gardens.

Gymnostoma sumatranum ■ Hill Rhu *(Rhu Bukit)*

DESCRIPTION Evergreen tree to 20m tall; crown conical when young, becoming roundish. Needle-shaped twigs, many short lateral branches, bushy, seldom exceeding 10cm long. Leaves scale-like in whorls of 4 at intervals of 0.2–0.3cm. Flowers minute, unisexual, with male and female flowers in different clusters. Male flowers in simple terminal spikes; female flowers in terminal heads. Fruits in cone-like heads, ellipsoid, *c.* 5cm across.

DISTRIBUTION AND ECOLOGY Sumatra and Borneo. Confined to hill, ridge and lower montane forests on ultramafic soils, and heath vegetation on sandstone. **USES** As an ornamental in streets and gardens.

CLUSIACEAE (MANGOSTEENS)

Garcinia atroviridis ■ *Asam gelugor*
(*Asam Keping*)

DESCRIPTION Medium-sized evergreen tree to 27m tall, with dense, narrowly conical crown. Leaves 14–28cm long, oblong to oblong-lanceolate, opposite. Male flowers 3–3.5cm long, bright red, in few-flowered clusters; female flowers solitary or rarely in pairs, red. Fruits to 8cm across, spherical or slightly flattened with 12–16 vertical furrows seated on persistent sepals and petals, ripening yellow to orange.

DISTRIBUTION AND ECOLOGY NE India, Myanmar, S Thailand and Peninsular Malaysia. Lowland evergreen forests. **USES** Widely cultivated for its sour fruits, the rind of which is sliced and dried, and used in curries or stewed with sugar as a dessert.

Garcinia cowa ■ *Kandis*

DESCRIPTION Small or medium-sized evergreen tree to 18m tall, with narrow crown. Leaves 6–13cm long, opposite, narrowly elliptic to oblong-lanceolate. Male flowers 1–1.4cm long, pale yellow or pink, solitary or in few-flowered clusters; female flowers c. 1.5cm across, solitary or 2–3 together in simple cluster, cream. Fruits to 3–8cm across, spherical or oval with 5–8 shallow grooves, seated on persistent sepals and petals, ripening yellow to orange. **DISTRIBUTION AND ECOLOGY** E to NE India, S China, Bangladesh, Andaman Islands, Myanmar, Thailand, Cambodia, Laos, Vietnam and Peninsular Malaysia. Lowland evergreen forests. **USES** Young leaves eaten as a vegetable, either raw or cooked. Fruits edible but very sour, and like those of *G. atroviridis* (see above), used to flavour curries or sour soups.

Garcinia hombroniana

■ Seashore Mangosteen (*Beruas*)

DESCRIPTION Small or medium-sized evergreen tree to 20m tall. Leaves 8–14cm long, ovate to elliptic-oblong, opposite. Male flowers 1.8–2.5cm across, creamy-white to pale yellow, in 3–6 flowered clusters; female flowers *c.* 2.5cm across, solitary. Fruits 3.5–5cm across, spherical, ripening pink to red.
DISTRIBUTION AND ECOLOGY Nicobar Islands to Peninsular Malaysia and Singapore. Lowland evergreen forests, often near coasts. **USES** Sometimes planted in villages for its edible fruits. White pulp is sourish-sweet.

Garcinia mangostana ■ Mangosteen (*Manggis*)

DESCRIPTION Small or medium-sized evergreen tree to 25m tall, with dense pyramidal or dome-like crown. Leaves 14–24cm long, opposite, elliptic-oblong. Female flowers *c*. 5cm across, solitary, dark pink to red-purple; male flowers unknown. Fruits 6–7cm across, globose, seated on persistent leathery sepals, dull red-purple to dark purplish-brown when ripe. **DISTRIBUTION AND ECOLOGY** Widely cultivated in SE Asia. Only known in cultivation. **USES** One of the most delicious local fruits, mostly eaten fresh.

COMBRETACEAE (SEA ALMONDS)

Terminalia calamansanai ■ Philippine Almond
(Kedah Tree, *Mentalun, Jelawai Mentalum*)

DESCRIPTION Deciduous tree to 30m tall; crown flat topped with steeply ascending main branches. Leaves 8–18cm long, crowded near ends of twigs, elliptic to obovate. Flowers c. 0.2cm across, cream or greenish-yellow, with strong, musty smell, in spikes 6–20cm long from leaf axils. Fruits 1.5–3cm long, hanging in tassels behind leaves, with varying shapes but with 2 broad side wings. **DISTRIBUTION AND ECOLOGY** Myanmar, Indo-China, Thailand, NW Peninsular Malaysia, the Philippines, SW Sulawesi, New Guinea and possibly Borneo. Common in open areas or on limestone outcrops. **USES** Sometimes grown as an ornamental street tree.

Terminalia catappa ■ Sea Almond
(Country Almond, Indian Almond, False Kamani, *Ketapang*)

DESCRIPTION Deciduous tree to 25m tall, pagoda shaped when young, with whorls of tiered branches; mature trees have stout crooked branches and irregular crown. Leaves 12–25cm long, obovate or elliptic; old leaves conspicuous when they turn orangish-yellow before falling. Flowers white or pale yellow-green, tiny; both male and female flowers in unbranched clusters 8–16cm long. Fruits 3.5–7cm long, ovoid or ellipsoid, slightly flattened, with stiff, narrow ridge along edge rather like an almond, green ripening yellow. **DISTRIBUTION AND ECOLOGY** India, and throughout SE Asia to N Australia and Polynesia. Common along sandy and rocky seashores. **USES** Commonly planted as a street tree throughout the tropics. Seeds edible and taste like almonds.

CYCADACEAE (CYCADS)

Cycas clivicola ■ Cliff Cycad
(*Paku Aji*)

DESCRIPTION Small tree to 8m tall, often with bulbous base; crown comprises tuft of leaves clustered near apex. Leaves pinnate, 70–165cm long, with 80–100 pairs of stiff leaflets. Trees unisexual. Male trees have terminal narrowly ovoid cone, 25–50cm long, microsporophylls 19–35mm long; female trees have megasporophylls to 15cm long in terminal overlapping cluster that before uncurling forms a cabbage-like dome. Seeds 40cm long, flattened ovoid, ripening yellow. **DISTRIBUTION AND ECOLOGY** N Peninsular Malaysia, peninsular and SW Thailand, S Vietnam and S Cambodia. Limestone hill outcrops. **USES** Planted as an ornamental, especially in Peninsular Malaysia and Thailand.

Cycas edentata ■ Sea Cycad (*Paku Laut*)

DESCRIPTION Small tree to 7m tall, with old trees branching without a swollen base; crown comprises tuft of leaves clustered near apex. Leaves pinnate, to 250cm long, with 25–90 pairs of stiff leaflets. Trees unisexual. Male trees have terminal narrowly ellipsoid to cylindric cone, to 40cm long, microsporophylls *c.* 40mm long; female trees have megasporophylls to 35cm long in loose, arching and pendulous clusters. Seeds 60–80cm long,

globose-ovoid, ripening reddish-brown. **DISTRIBUTION AND ECOLOGY** Andaman Islands, S Myanmar, Thailand, S Vietnam, Singapore, Sumatra, Java, N Borneo and the C and W Philippines. Coastal areas, usually on shallow, poor substrates on sandy beaches or on bare granite rock. **USES** Very popular as an ornamental – particularly old, branched specimens that are collected from the wild for use in landscaping.

DILLENIACEAE (DILLENIAS)

Dillenia excelsa ■ Simpoh

DESCRIPTION Evergreen tree to 40m tall, with dense, rounded crown. Leaves 15–30cm long, elliptic to oblong, often asymmetric, margin shallow toothed. Flowers 7–10cm across, bright yellow with red-purple stamens, in terminal branched clusters of 3–12 upwards-facing flowers. Fruits *c.* 5cm across, red to white, splitting open

into star-like structure with 5–9 spreading, boat-shaped segments. **DISTRIBUTION AND ECOLOGY** S Thailand, Peninsular Malaysia, Sumatra, Java and Borneo. Lowland evergreen forests. **USES** Sometimes planted as an ornamental street tree.

Dillenia indica ■ Indian Simpoh
(Elephant Apple, *Simpoh Ayer*)

DESCRIPTION Evergreen tree to 25m tall, with stout, spreading branches. Leaves 15–30cm long, narrowly elliptic-oblong, margin serrated. Flowers  15–20cm across, white with pale orange stamens, solitary at ends of branches, hanging face down. Fruits 8–10cm across, spherical, enclosed by thick sepals, bright green ripening yellow-green, not splitting open. **DISTRIBUTION AND ECOLOGY** India, Myanmar, S China, Indo-China, Thailand, Peninsular Malaysia, Borneo, Sumatra and Java. Common along streams. **USES** Sometimes planted as an ornamental street tree.

Dillenia ovata ■ Sacred Simpoh
(Kedah Simpoh, *Simpoh Beludu*)

DESCRIPTION Evergreen tree to 25m tall with dense bushy crown. Leaves 10–24cm long, oval to elliptic ovate, velvety hairy below, slightly asymmetric, margin finely toothed. Flowers *c.* 16cm across, bright yellow, terminal and solitary. Fruits 5–6cm across, spherical, not splitting, green ripening dull yellow. **DISTRIBUTION AND ECOLOGY** S Thailand, Peninsular Malaysia, Sumatra and Banka. Lowland freshwater swamps to evergreen forest. **USES** Sometimes planted as an ornamental street tree. Timber used for beams, planks and furniture, and suitable for musical instruments such as clappers.

Dillenia philippinensis
■ Philippine Simpoh (*Katmon*)

DESCRIPTION Small evergreen tree to 15m tall, with thick, bushy crown. Leaves 8–25cm long, elliptic to oblong-ovate, margins serrated. Flowers white, 10–25cm across, with purple stamens, upwards-facing, solitary or in 2–3 flowered clusters. Fruits 5–6cm across, globose. **DISTRIBUTION AND ECOLOGY** Endemic in the Philippines, where it grows along riverbanks of lowland forests. **USES** Fruits, young shoots and flowers used in flavouring dishes. Often planted as an ornamental.

Dillenia suffruticosa ■ Shrubby Simpoh (*Simpoh Ayer*)

DESCRIPTION Large evergreen shrub or small tree to 8m tall and forming thicket. Leaves

15–30cm long, elliptic to obovate, margin with shallow teeth. Flowers 8–12cm across, yellow with yellow stamens, in branched clusters of 3–12 downwards-facing flowers. Fruits *c.* 5cm across, 5–8 carpels splitting into open, star-shaped structure when ripe, pink to dull red. Seeds covered with red aril. **DISTRIBUTION AND ECOLOGY** Peninsular Malaysia, Sumatra and Borneo. Naturalized in Sri Lanka, Thailand, W Java and the Philippines. Secondary forests and swampy habitats. **USES** Planted as an ornamental.

EBENACEAE (EBONY AND PERSIMMON)

Diospyros discolor ▪ Velvet Persimmon
(Butter Fruit, *Mabolo*, *Buah Lemak*, *Buah Mentega*, *Kamagong*)

DESCRIPTION Medium-sized evergreen tree to 18m tall, with conical crown. Leaves 10–22cm long, oblong, lower surface silvery hairy. Flowers unisexual, with male and female flowers on different trees. Male flowers *c.* 1.8cm diameter, in 3–7-flowered axillary clusters; female flowers solitary, slightly larger than male flowers. Fruits to 8cm diameter, solitary, unstalked, globose or slightly flattened, densely covered with fine silvery or brownish hairs, ripening to peach colour or brownish-red. **DISTRIBUTION AND ECOLOGY** Endemic in the Philippines, where it grows in lowland monsoon climate at low and medium altitudes. **USES** Cultivated as a fruit tree; fruits eaten fresh when ripe with a cheese-like odour. Wood durable, smooth and black, and often used in making handicrafts.

Diospyros malabarica ▪ Malabar Ebony (Indian Persimmon, *Komoi*, *Kumun*)

DESCRIPTION Small to medium-sized evergreen tree 15–35m tall, with low, bushy, thick, rounded crown. Leaves 7–32cm long, oblanceolate. Flowers unisexual, with male and female flowers on different trees; creamy-white, fragrant, borne on leafy shoots. Fruits globose, 5–7.5cm across, covered with velvety hairs, brown ripening red. **DISTRIBUTION AND ECOLOGY** India, Sri Lanka, Myanmar, Thailand, Peninsular Malaysia and Indonesia. Lowland forests, often near streams. **USES** Unripe fruits and leaves used to extract tannin to dye cloth black and tan nets and hides. Wood used for furniture and handicrafts. Fruits edible. Occasionally planted as an ornamental.

ELAEOCARPACEAE

Elaeocarpus grandiflorus ■ Fairy Petticoat (Lily of the Valley Tree, *Mala*)

DESCRIPTION Small to medium-sized evergreen tree to 20m tall. Leaves 6–18cm long, lanceolate, pinkish when young; mature leaves before being shed turn red, margin toothed. Pendulous flowers in clusters, pinkish-red sepals and white-fringed petals, 1.5–2.5cm long. Fruits pendulous, green, ellipsoid, 2.5–4cm long, with hard ellipsoid stone. Flowers and fruits both very attractive. **DISTRIBUTION AND ECOLOGY** Myanmar, Thailand, Indo-China, Peninsular Malaysia, Sumatra, Java, Bali, Borneo and the Philippines. Lowland to hill forests to 1,200m elevation, sometimes along streams. **USES** In recent years has been introduced as an ornamental tree, more so in Thailand than elsewhere.

Elaeocarpus petiolatus ■ Board-leafed Oil Fruit (*Mendong*)

DESCRIPTION Small to medium-sized evergreen tree to
21m tall, with spreading crown. Leaves entire with long
petiole up to 8cm long, blade 10–25cm long, elliptic to
oblong. Inflorescences in racemes clustered near apex
of twigs. Flowers white, *c.* 1.2cm long, petals fringed.
Fruits ellipsoid to oblong, *c.* 1.5cm long, green ripening
blue with oily pulp. **DISTRIBUTION AND ECOLOGY**
Widespread from India to Indo-China and Hainan,
to Sumatra, Java and Borneo. Common in lowland
secondary and primary forests.

Elaeocarpus robustus var. *megacarpus* ■ Ceylon Olive (*Indian Olive*)

DESCRIPTION Evergreen tree to 25m tall.
Leaves 8–25cm long, ovate to elliptic, margin
wavy, shallowly rounded teeth. Flowers 1–1.3cm
across, white, in dense racemes at leaf axils, petals
deeply and finely fringed. Fruits 5–7cm long,
spherical to oval or ellipsoid, ripening olive-
green to yellowish-brown, endocarp smooth.
DISTRIBUTION AND ECOLOGY Peninsular
Malaysia and Sumatra. Lowland to lower montane
evergreen forests.

EUPHORBIACEAE (RUBBER AND SPURGES)

Aleurites moluccana
■ Candlenut Tree (Kekui Nut Tree, *Buah Keras*)

DESCRIPTION Evergreen tree to 25m tall, with spreading crown. Leaves 10–28cm long, triangular or ovate. Flowers white or cream, in branched, many-flowered clusters; male and female on same cluster. Male flowers 5–10mm long, white to cream; female flowers slightly larger than male flowers. Fruits 5–7cm across, green with whitish flesh, broadly ovoid to spherical. **DISTRIBUTION AND ECOLOGY** Country of origin unknown; only known in cultivation. Grown throughout the tropics. **USES** Nuts often used in SE Asian cuisine, to thicken sauces; they are mildly toxic when raw. In the past, the high oil content of the nut was used for an oil burnt for light. Oil is also extracted for making soap and candles, hence the English name Candlenut Tree.

Hevea brasiliensis ■ Rubber Tree

DESCRIPTION Deciduous tree to 25m
tall. Leaves trifoliate, leaflets 5–21cm long.
Flowers yellow, fragrant, unisexual together
in branched clusters to 30cm long. Fruits *c*.
5cm across, strongly 3-lobed, leathery, bony
when ripe, splitting into 3 parts with 1 large
seed in each segment. **DISTRIBUTION AND
ECOLOGY** Lowland forests of tropical S
America. **USES** One of the most important
industrial crop trees for Thailand, Indonesia
and Malaysia. Produces natural rubber. Timber
widely used in furniture making.

Hura crepitans ■ Sandbox Tree
(Monkey's Dinner Bell, Huru, Pin Wheel Tree)

DESCRIPTION
Evergreen tree to 15m tall, with whorled horizontal branches when young, developing into dense, spreading crown. Trunk spiny when young. Leaves 7–21cm long, ovate to elliptic with cordate bases, margin entire to finely toothed. Flowers unisexual with solitary female flowers and dense clusters of male flowers. Fruits 5–8cm across, pale green ripening red-brown, flattened-spherical with many distinct grooves, becoming hard, dehiscing open when ripe. **DISTRIBUTION AND ECOLOGY** Tropical America. Moist coastal forests and rainforests. **USES** Cultivated throughout the tropics as an ornamental.

Macaranga gigantea ■ *Mahang Gajah*

DESCRIPTION Small tree to 15m tall, with open, irregularly shaped crown. Leaves to 60cm long, trilobed, deeply peltate. Male flowers in dense, branched clusters, grey, hairy; female flowers in similar clusters but smaller. Fruits *c.* 8cm long, strongly 2-lobed, yellow without spines or horns. **DISTRIBUTION AND ECOLOGY** S Thailand, Peninsular Malaysia, Sumatra, Borneo and Sulawesi. Common in moist secondary growth.

Macaranga tanarius ■ *Mahang*

DESCRIPTION Small tree to 12m tall, with bushy, rounded crown. Leaves 8–22cm long, not lobed, ovate, distinctly peltate. Male flowers in much-branched clusters; clusters of female flowers less branched. Fruits to 6cm long, globose, with many slender, tentacle-like soft spines, covered with pale grey or yellowish powdery wax. **DISTRIBUTION AND ECOLOGY** India, Andaman and Nicobar Islands, S China, Taiwan, through SE Asia to Melanesia and Australia. Secondary growth and gaps in evergreen forests.

FABACEAE (LEGUMES)

Acacia auriculiformis ■ Northern Black Wattle
(Acacia Tree, Ear-leaved Acacia)

DESCRIPTION Evergreen tree to 30m tall, diameter of more than 50cm. Trunk often has low branches. Leaves simple phyllodes (petioles changing into leaf-like structure), distinctly curved, *c.* 10–16cm long. Flowers in slender spikes, *c.* 10cm long, with short main stalk, yellow. Fruits flattened in strongly contorted coils, 2.5–4cm diameter; seeds black encircled by orange aril. **DISTRIBUTION AND ECOLOGY** Moluccas, New Guinea and N Australia. Estimated to range from subtropical moist to wet forests, through tropical dry to wet forests. **USES** Grown as a fast-growing tree in plantations. Widely planted as an ornamental and often naturalized in open areas.

Acacia mangium ■ Black Wattle (Acacia, Hickory Wattle, Mangium)

DESCRIPTION Evergreen tree to 30m tall, diameter of more than 70cm, crown spreading. Leaves simple phyllodes (petioles changing into leaf-like structure), distinctly curved, *c.* 20–26cm long. Flowers in slender spikes, *c.* 8–11cm long, with short main stalk, yellow. Fruits flattened, irregularly coiled, *c.* 10cm long; seeds black with fleshy folded aril. **DISTRIBUTION AND ECOLOGY** Indonesian islands of S Moluccas, Sulawesi and Aru, New Guinea and NE Australia. Often in grassland and on margins of lowland primary forests, from tropical dry and moist subtropical dry forests, to wet forests. **USES** Extremely fast-growing tree, widely planted in plantations for both pulp and paper, and timber. Occasionally planted as an ornamental tree.

Adenanthera pavonina ■ Tree Peacock (Coral Bean Tree, Redwood, *Saga*)

DESCRIPTION Deciduous tree to 25m tall, with irregular, rounded crown. Leaves bipinnately compound, 3–6 pairs of opposite pinnae 8–20cm long. Flowers in 12–30cm-long spikes; creamy-yellow, *c.* 1cm long. Fruits pale green ripening brown to blackish, strap shaped, curved slightly and becoming spirally twisted after dehiscing, revealing uniformly red, smooth, heart-shaped seeds. **DISTRIBUTION AND ECOLOGY** Thailand, Malaysia and Indonesia. Lowland and coastal evergreen forests. **USES** Widely planted as a street tree in the tropics. Red seeds sometimes collected and used as beads in jewellery.

Albizia saman ■ Raintree
(Monkey-pod Tree, Cow Tamarind, Five O'clock Tree, *Hujan Hujan*)

DESCRIPTION Deciduous tree to 60m tall, diameter of more than 2m, with large, symmetrical, umbrella-shaped spreading crown. Leaves bipinnately compound with 3–9 pairs of leaflets. Leaflets close up at dusk (at five o'clock) or before a storm, hence the name 'rain tree'. Flowers pink to red-purple in simple heads on slender stalks. Fruits are flattened pods, 20–30cm long, ripening black. **DISTRIBUTION AND ECOLOGY** Yucatan Peninsula and Guatemala, to Peru, Bolivia and Brazil. Ranges from subtropical very dry and moist forests, to tropical dry and moist forests. **USES** Widely planted as a street tree. Timber used in furniture, carvings and panelling.

Amherstia nobilis ■ Pride of Burma (Noble Amherstia)

DESCRIPTION Evergreen tree to 10–15m tall; branched trunk with rounded crown and gently weeping branches. Leaves pinnately compound without terminal leaflets, 14–34cm long, each leaf with *c*. 6–8 leaflets; young leaves pendent and pinkish-coppery in colour. Inflorescence on terminal pendulous racemes with 20–26 flowers. Flowers have 5 petals, asymmetric, red to crimson; largest petal erect with yellow patch at apex. Pod flattened and woody, red with pale yellow patches ripening brown, 11–20cm long. **DISTRIBUTION AND ECOLOGY** Genus with a single species, native in Myanmar, and very rare in the wild. Lowland monsoon teak forests on calcareous soil. **USES** Beautiful tree with most attractive flowers. Seeds often hard to obtain, so not as widely planted as could be expected.

Andira inermis

■ Brown Heart
(Cabbage Tree, Bastard Mahogany, Crown Heart)

DESCRIPTION
Deciduous tree to 20m tall, sometimes taller. Leaves pinnately compound with terminal leaflets, 7–17 leaflets, 15–40cm long. Flowers in dense terminal clusters, dark pink to purplish-red, *c.* 1cm long. Flowering often preceded by leaf fall and flushes of new growth. Whole crown is then flushed with purple blooms. Fruits are 1-seeded pods, 4–8cm long, oval in shape.
DISTRIBUTION AND ECOLOGY Tropical America. Common in riparian zones and areas with high water table. Evergreen tropical rainforests to dry savannah vegetation.
USES Widely planted as an ornamental.

Archidendron clypearia ■ Greater Grasshopper Tree
(*Petai Belalang, Chahar*)

DESCRIPTION Small tree to 15m tall. Leaves bipinnate, pinnae 4–9, main stalk 15–50cm long. Flowers in large terminal cluster, white to cream, to 13mm long. Fruits flattened, spirally twisted, ripening bright red. **DISTRIBUTION AND ECOLOGY** Four varieties found in SE Asia. Widespread in lowland forests.

Archidendron ellipticum ■ *Saga Gajah (Jiring Tupai, Kabau, Kenoah)*

DESCRIPTION Small tree to 20m tall. Leaves bipinnate with 1(2) pairs of pinnae; main stalk 5–15cm long. Flowers pale yellow in small heads grouped in branched clusters. Fruits tightly twisted in coil, *c*. 7.5–9cm across, dull red dehiscing and exposing black seeds dangling on strings. **DISTRIBUTION AND ECOLOGY** Native in peninsular Thailand, Malaysia, Indonesia and the Philippines. Common in forests and open areas, often by the sea near rocky headlands.

Archidendron jiringa ■ *Jering*

DESCRIPTION Small tree to 15m tall. Leaves bipinnate, 1 pair of pinnae to 20cm long, each with 2–3 pairs of opposite leaflets. Flowers greenish-white to cream in small heads, grouped in branched clusters to 30cm long on leaf axils of older stems. Fruits *c*. 25cm long, spirally twisted or contorted, strap shaped with swellings over seeds, dark brown to

purple-brown. **DISTRIBUTION AND ECOLOGY** Bangladesh, Myanmar, Thailand, Peninsular Malaysia, Sumatra, Banka, Java and Borneo. Lowland evergreen forests – both primary and secondary. **USES** Often planted in villages for its edible seeds. These should be cooked before eating because they contain toxins that break down with cooking.

Brownea ariza
■ Scarlet Flame Bean
(Rose of Venezuela, Handkerchief Tree)

DESCRIPTION Evergreen small tree to 7–9m tall, shrubby in habit with low, dense, rounded crown. Leaves pinnately compound with 5–7 leaflets, *c.* 18–25cm long; young leaves pendulous, light brown. Inflorescence 9–10cm diameter. Flowers in dense clusters, ovoid, red with yellow anthers, 3.5–4cm long. Fruits in pods *c.* 15cm long. **DISTRIBUTION AND ECOLOGY** Colombia and Venezuela. Tropical rainforests. **USES** Sometimes cultivated as an ornamental tree.

Brownea grandiceps ■ Rose of Venezuela
(Rose of the Mountain, Scarlet Flame Bean)

DESCRIPTION Evergreen tree to 20m tall; branched trunk with dense, rounded crown with pendulous branches. Leaves pinnately compound with 8–12 pairs of leaflets, *c.* 20–30cm long; young leaves pendulous, attractive brown with green speckles. Flowers in dense globular clusters; red petals with yellow stamens, *c.* 5– 8cm long. Fruits in long, brown, furry pods. **DISTRIBUTION AND ECOLOGY** Native in Brazil, Ecuador, Honduras, Venezuela and Colombia in tropical rainforests. **USES** Sometimes planted as an ornamental, although not very popular.

Calliandra haematocephala ■ Red Powderpuff
(Blood-red Tassel-flower, Pink Powderpuff)

DESCRIPTION Shrub to small tree to 5m tall, with spreading, rounded crown. Leaves up to 14cm long, bipinnate, 1–3 pairs of pinnae, 7–10 pairs of leaflets. Flowers in heads of bright red stamens, 7–10cm diameter. Fruits are flattened pods with thickened edges, *c.* 10cm long, dehiscent. **DISTRIBUTION AND ECOLOGY** Tropical S America. Lowland open areas and savannah. **USES** Widely cultivated as an ornamental shrub.

Calliandra tergemina var. *emerginata*
■ Dwarf Powderpuff (Red Powderpuff, Miniature Powderpuff)

DESCRIPTION Similar to *C. haematocephala* (see above), but leaves smaller with 3 leaflets (2 paired terminal ones, 1 lone and smaller one) per petiole. Flowers smaller, 2.5–6cm across. **DISTRIBUTION AND ECOLOGY** Mexico, Central America, Venezuela and Colombia. Secondary forests. **USES** Widely cultivated as an ornamental bush.

Cassia fistula ■ Golden Shower (Indian Laburnum, *Busu Busu*)

DESCRIPTION Medium-sized deciduous tree to 20m tall, with slender, drooping branches. Leaves 12– 40cm long with 3–8 pairs of leaflets. Flowers very showy, 3.5–5cm long, golden yellow, in pendulous, unbranched clusters 20–60cm long. Fruits tubular, green ripening black, 20–60cm long. **DISTRIBUTION AND ECOLOGY** Probably native in deciduous forests of India, Sri Lanka, Myanmar, Thailand and Indonesia. Dry deciduous forests of lower altitudes. **USES** Widely cultivated as a street tree for its regular, spectacular yellow blooms.

Cassia javanica ■ Pink Shower (Java Cassia, Apple Blossom Shower)

DESCRIPTION Attractive small to medium-sized deciduous or semi-deciduous tree, 15m tall. Inflorescence clusters terminal on leafy shoots or lateral on short side branches, up to 16cm long, many flowered; flowers whitish to reddish or buff. In places with a distinct dry season, crown blossoms with pink flowers after leaf fall. Fruits pendent, cylindrical, 20–60cm long. **DISTRIBUTION AND ECOLOGY** India, Myanmar, Thailand, Peninsular Malaysia, Indonesia and the Philippines. Low elevations in open sites in evergreen and deciduous monsoon forests, or even in savannah-like vegetation. **USES** Often in cultivation as a wayside tree. Species is rather polymorphic and several subspecies are found SE Asia. All have attractive flowers and all are found in cultivation, but the subspecies *javanica* is the one most often grown.

Clitoria fairchildiana ■ Butterfly Pea Tree
(Orchid Tree, Philippine Pigeonwings)

DESCRIPTION Small to medium-sized deciduous tree to 15m tall, with low, branching and pendulous branches. Crown bushy and rounded. Leaves trifoliate. Flowers in pendent clusters, pale violet, pea-like, slightly fragrant. Fruits in long, woody pods, green maturing brown. **DISTRIBUTION AND ECOLOGY** N Brazil. Rainforests, mainly in open areas of secondary growth. **USES** Widely planted as a street tree for its dense crown and attractive flowers.

Cynometra cauliflora ■ *Namnam* (*Katak Puru, Puki Anjing, Namu Namu*)

DESCRIPTION Small evergreen tree with dense crown, 3–15m tall. Leaves have 1 pair of leaflets with strongly asymmetric base. Flowers cauliflorous (flowers on main trunk), in short, unbranched clusters; flowers *c.* 1.2cm long, white. Fruits 3–6cm long, hanging from main trunk, kidney shaped, knobby, pale brown to yellowish, with firm, apple-like texture when ripe. **DISTRIBUTION AND ECOLOGY** Only known from planted trees in SE Asia, India and Sri Lanka. Probably native in eastern SE Asia. **USES** There are both sour and sweet varieties. Pods eaten raw or cooked.

Dalbergia cochinchinensis

■ Siamese Rosewood (Trac, Tracwood, *Hongmu*)

DESCRIPTION Evergreen tree to *c*. 30m tall, with thick crown. Leaves 13–25cm long with 3–4 pairs of leaflets. Flowers at ends of branched clusters, *c*. 0.6cm long, white tinged pale yellow inside. Fruit a flat pod, indehiscent, with 1–3 seeds, pale green ripening pale brown. **DISTRIBUTION AND ECOLOGY** Thailand, Cambodia, Laos and Vietnam. Lowland deciduous forests. **USES** Occasionally planted as a street tree. Timber highly valued, threatening the native population of this species with illegal logging and trafficking.

Delonix regia

■ Flame of the Forest (Red Flame,
Phoenix Tree, Royal Poinciana,
Flamboyant Tree, *Semarak Api*)

DESCRIPTION Small deciduous
tree, 9–10m tall with umbrella-
shaped crown. Leaves bipinnately
compound, 20–60cm long. Flowers
in terminal clusters, bright red and
orange, 10–13cm across. Fruits
a pod, flattened, green ripening
reddish-brown to black, woody, 30–
75cm long. **DISTRIBUTION AND
ECOLOGY** Endemic to Madagascar
in dry deciduous forest. Endangered
in the wild. **USES** Widely
cultivated for its brilliant red
flowers. In regions with a distinct
dry season, the crown blossoms
with spectacular red flowers. There
is a yellow-flowered variety.

Erythrina crista-galli
■ Coral Tree (*Cockspur Coral Tree*)

DESCRIPTION
Small deciduous tree to 15m tall. Leaves trifoliate, leaflets *c.* 4–9cm long. Flowers *c.* 5cm long, in terminal racemes, dark crimson. Fruits curved, strap-shaped pods, rather constricted in between seeds, 10–18cm long. **DISTRIBUTION AND ECOLOGY** S America; Argentina, Uruguay, Paraguay, Brazil and Bolivia. Swampy or wet soils in grassland and in files, often bordering rivers and estuaries. **USES** Frequently planted as a street tree. The national flower of Argentina.

Falcataria mollucana ■ Moluccan Albizia
(Falcata, Albizia, *Batai, Sengon, Salawaku, Sau*)

DESCRIPTION Fast-growing deciduous tree to 40m tall, with spreading, flat crown. Leaves bipinnate with 8–12 pairs of pinnae, 8–18 pairs of opposite leaflets. Flowers white to cream, in branched clusters, solitary or in loose groups. Fruits 8–13cm long, pale brown, oblong, straight, flat. **DISTRIBUTION AND ECOLOGY** Moluccas, New Guinea, Bismarck Archipelago and Solomon Islands, where it is a pioneer species in lowland rainforests and secondary vegetation. Naturalized in many tropical countries. **USES** Often planted as a fast-growing plantation tree for its soft timber and use in paper pulp. Sometimes used as an ornamental in parks.

Gliricidia sepium
■ Mexican Lilac (Mother of Cocoa)

DESCRIPTION Small deciduous tree to
12m tall, with irregularly spreading crown.
Leaves 15–35cm long, with 5–8 pairs of
opposite leaflets and terminal leaflet. Flowers
c. 2cm long, pale pink or lilac with yellow
patch at base. Fruits 10–18cm long, narrowly
elliptic, flattened. **DISTRIBUTION AND
ECOLOGY** Central America; Costa Rica,
north to Mexico. Secondary lowland forests
and disturbed sites. **USES** Often planted as a
village tree; sometimes used as a living fence.
In cacao plantations, planted to provide
partial shade to cacao bushes.

Leucaena leucocephala

■ *Horse Tamarind* (Leucaena, *Ipil Ipil, Petai Jawa*)

DESCRIPTION Tree to 10m tall, with open crown and feathery foliage. Leaves bipinnate with 4–8 pairs of pinnae, *c.* 10cm long. Flowers in dense, spherical heads on slender, hairy stalk. Fruits in flattened pods, green ripening brown, 12–20cm long. **DISTRIBUTION AND ECOLOGY** Native in tropical America. Dry coastal regions and waste ground.

Naturalized in most of SE Asia. **USES** Widely planted as a multi-purpose tree for fuel, fodder for livestock and reforestation programmes. In Thailand, young shoots and green pods are eaten as a vegetable.

Maniltoa lenticellata

■ Cascading Maniltoa (Cascading Bean, Silk Handkerchief Tree)

DESCRIPTION Evergreen tree to 42m tall, with spreading, rounded crown and thick foliage. Leaves *c.* 30cm long, even-pinnate, 4–5 pairs, asymmetric at bases. Flowers white, clustered on dense, head-like clusters 3–6cm wide with many brown bracts at base. Fruits 2.5–4cm long, obliquely oval or ovoid, slightly flattened, thick skinned, smooth or shallowly wrinkled, covered with orange-brown scales. **DISTRIBUTION AND ECOLOGY** Papua New Guinea and Australia (Queensland). Understorey tree of lowland evergreen forests. **USES** Sometimes planted as an ornamental. Makes a good shade tree. Flowers synchronously, with crown flushed with white-flowered clusters.

Millettia pinnata ■ Indian Beech
(Pongam Oil Tree, *Mempari*)

DESCRIPTION
Deciduous tree to
15m tall, with short,
stout trunk and
spreading branches.
Leaves pinnate with
2(–3) pairs of leaflets
with terminal leaflet,
15–30cm long.
Flowers in slender
racemes at leaf axils,
1.2–1.5cm long, white
to lilac. Fruits 4–8cm
long, oblong with
short, curved tip. **DISTRIBUTION AND ECOLOGY** Occurs
naturally or locally naturalized from Pakistan, India and Sri
Lanka, throughout SE Asia, to Japan, N Australia and Fiji.
Common along coasts and riverbanks. **USES** Frequently
planted as an ornamental. Previously known as *Pongamia
pinnata* and only recently transferred to the genus *Millettia*.

Parkia speciosa ■ *Petai*

DESCRIPTION Large deciduous
tree to 40m tall, with spreading
crown, often with prominent
buttresses. Leaves bipinnate
with 11–20 pairs of pinnae;
leaflets tiny. Flowers 6–10mm
long, in dense, club-shaped head
on long, pendulous stalk. Each
head has fluffy white sterile
flowers at the base, a band of
nectar-bearing female flowers in the centre and a dense
mass of yellow bisexual flowers towards the top. Fruits
36–45cm long, green, several hanging from end of swollen common stalk; strap shaped,
usually spirally twisted, swollen over seeds and constricted in between. Seeds remain soft
at maturity. **DISTRIBUTION AND ECOLOGY** S Thailand, Peninsular Malaysia, Borneo
and the Philippines (Palawan). Lowland evergreen forests. **USES** Seeds widely eaten, with a
strongly garlic smell.

Peltophorum pterocarpum ■ Yellow Flame
(*Jemerlang*, *Batai Laut*, Yellow Poinciana, Copperpod, Rusty Shield)

DESCRIPTION Deciduous or semi-evergreen tree with dense, dome-shaped crown. Leaves bipinnate with 4–14 pairs of pinnae, each with 9–20 pairs of leaflets. Flowers *c.* 3.5cm long in large terminal pyramidal clusters, bright yellow. Fruits 6–12cm long, flattened, with narrow papery wings along edges, ripening purple-brown with 1–5 pale brown seeds.
DISTRIBUTION AND ECOLOGY India and Sri Lanka, through SE Asia to N Australia. Frequently found in coastal habitats along beaches and behind mangroves. **USES** Widely cultivated throughout SE Asia as an ornamental tree.

Pithecellobium dulce ■ Madras Thorn
(Manila Tamarind, *Asam Keranji*)

DESCRIPTION Evergreen tree to 15m tall, with dense, bushy crown. Twigs armed with pairs of spines at leaf bases. Leaves bipinnate with only 1 pair of leaflets, 1.5–5cm long. Flowers cream to greenish-white, in heads of 8–20 uniform flowers along a rachis. Fruits 10–15cm long, spirally coiled into a circle, *c.* 5cm across, green flushed pink, eventually splitting open at both ends; seeds black with fleshy white or pinkish aril. **DISTRIBUTION AND ECOLOGY** C and S America. Dry, brushy or thinly forested plains or hillsides, often in coastal thickets at low elevations. Sometimes naturalized in open areas. **USES** Cultivated as an ornamental and for edible arils.

Pterocarpus indicus
■ Angsana (Amboyna Wood, Philippine Mahogany, *Sena*, *Narra*)

DESCRIPTION Large deciduous tree, reaching over 30m in height, with diameter exceeding 2m in old trees. Leaves compound, 20–50cm long; leaflets mostly 7–9. Flowers 1.5cm long, ochre-yellow, very fragrant, in axillary racemes 15–30cm long. Pods flattened dorsoventrally, semi-orbicular with a lateral point, 4–6cm in diameter. Magnificent tree, periodically blooming, when whole crown turns yellow. The display lasts a few days, often carpeting the floor with fallen yellow petals. **DISTRIBUTION AND ECOLOGY** SE Asia, S China, Ryukyu Islands, N Australia and Solomon Islands. Often in coastal vegetation. **USES** Very popular roadside tree, especially in Penang; some of the old trees are very large, with many exceeding 150cm diameter. Timber makes very fine furniture.

Saraca cauliflora ■ Yellow Saraca (Yellow Asoka, *Gapis*)

DESCRIPTION Medium-sized evergreen tree to *c*. 20m tall, with dense, spreading crown. Leaves with 5–7 pairs of leaflets, 25–80cm long; young pendulous flushes of leaves purplish-red before stiffening upon maturation. Flowers pale orange-yellow, usually with red eye, in dense clusters, 15–40cm wide, mostly on main trunk and larger limbs. Fruits in large flattened pods, 30–45cm long, purple to rich red-brown, with 6–8 seeds in each pod. **DISTRIBUTION AND ECOLOGY** Myanmar, Thailand, Peninsular Malaysia and Java. Locally abundant along streams and small rivers under shade. **USES** Often planted as a street tree.

Saraca declinata ■ Red Saraca (*Gapis*)

DESCRIPTION Shrub or small tree to 12m tall, with a rather loose crown. Leaves with 3–5 pairs of leaflets, 15–50cm long. Flowers in much-branched clusters 5–30cm across, among or behind leaves on branches, yellow turning pink, then red with darker eye. Fruits in clusters of up to 9 pods, oblong to lanceolate with straight or curved beak, ripening dark brown, 10–30cm long. **DISTRIBUTION AND ECOLOGY** Myanmar, Thailand, Cambodia, Laos, Vietnam, Peninsular Malaysia, Sumatra, Riau, Lingga, Anambas, Borneo, E Java and Flores. Common in lowland forests and often gregarious along streams. **USES** Occasionally planted as an ornamental.

Sesbania grandiflora

■ Vegetable Hummingbird (Scarlet Wisteria Tree, West Indian Pea Tree, *Petai Belalang*)

DESCRIPTION Fast-growing evergreen shrub or small tree to 8m tall. Leaves 15–30cm long, with 10–20 pairs or more of leaflets. Flowers very large and showy, 5–8cm long, creamy-white to pink or deep red. Fruits 30–45cm long, narrowly cylindrical, slightly flattened.
DISTRIBUTION AND ECOLOGY Origin unknown; probably native in SE Asia. Dry wasteland and roadsides. **USES** Widely cultivated for its edible flowers.

Senna alata

■ Seven Golden Candlestick (Candle Bush, Christmas Candle, Ringworm Cassia)

DESCRIPTION Shrub 2–5m tall, with stout, spreading branches. Leaves 30–60cm long with 8–20 pairs of leaflets, without a terminal leaflet. Flowers in terminal spike, bright yellow, *c.* 2cm long, bud protected by bright orange-brown bract. Fruits 10–16cm long, squarish in section, with 4 narrow wings. **DISTRIBUTION AND ECOLOGY** S America, naturalized in SE Asia. Often found in disturbed habitat. **USES** Leaves and plant sap have anti-fungal properties and are sometimes used to treat ringworm infections. Leaves are poisonous and can be a problem for livestock. Widely cultivated throughout the tropics.

Senna multijuga

■ False Sicklepod (November Shower)

DESCRIPTION Small tree to *c.* 10m tall, with slender branches and flattened, fern-like foliage. Leaves 15–22cm long, 18–30 pairs of leaflets with distinctive conical nectary between lowest pair of leaflets. Flowers *c.* 3cm long, golden yellow, in terminal branched clusters of flowers. Fruits strap shaped with raised lines, 30–60 seeds per pod. **DISTRIBUTION AND ECOLOGY** Native in northern parts of S America. Open areas and savannah to rainforests. **USES** Cultivated widely in SE Asia as an attractive ornamental; sometimes naturalized but can become invasive.

Senna siamea ■ Siamese Senna
(Kassod Tree, *Johar*, *Johor*)

DESCRIPTION Evergreen tree to 20m tall, with rounded or irregular crown. Leaves 15–30cm long with 7– 10 pairs of leaflets. Flowers 2.5–37.7cm long, bright yellow, in clusters at ends of twigs. Fruits 15–30cm long, slightly curved, flattened with wavy surface, strap shaped. **DISTRIBUTION AND ECOLOGY** Myanmar, Thailand, Indo-China and possibly northern Peninsular Malaysia. Widespread in secondary growth and open areas. **USES** Often cultivated in villages as an ornamental.

Senna spectabilis ■ Spectacular Cassia
(American Cassia, Popcorn Tree, Weeping Cassia)

DESCRIPTION Small tree to *c.* 18m tall, with sprawling, long, slender branches. Leaves 20–35cm long, 10–15 leaflets, minutely hairy below. Flowers 2–3.5cm long, yellow, on terminal clusters 20–60cm long held upright. Fruits 18–25cm long, cylindrical, pendulous, green ripening glossy black, 50–70 seeds per pod. **DISTRIBUTION AND ECOLOGY** Native in tropical America. Dry-land forests and open areas, disturbed and secondary woodland and savannah. Often naturalized on waste ground. **USES** Commonly planted in SE Asia as an attractive ornamental.

Tamarindus indica ■ Tamarind (*Assam Jawa*)

DESCRIPTION Deciduous tree to 30m tall. Leaves 8–16cm long, with 10–18 pairs of leaflets without terminal leaflet. Flowers in loose clusters, petals pale yellow with red veins. Fruits 5–15cm long, pendulous, oblong, straight to curved, shallowly constricted between brown seeds. **DISTRIBUTION AND ECOLOGY** Probably native in E Africa. Low-altitude woodland, savannah and bush. Occasionally naturalized. **USES**

Widely cultivated in the tropics for fruits. Sour pulp from fruits commonly used to flavour soups and curries. An important ingredient in many SE Asian dishes. Sweet variety cultivated in Thailand is eaten as a fresh fruit.

GENTIANACEAE (GENTIANS)

Cyrtophyllum fragrans ■ *Tembusu*

DESCRIPTION
Evergreen tree to 30m tall, with dense conical crown; bark deeply and irregularly fissured. Leaves 7.5–13cm long, opposite, elliptic. Flowers 1.4–2.3cm long, in branched

clusters, creamy-white to pale yellow. Fruits 0.5–1cm long, spherical or ovoid, ripening orange or red. **DISTRIBUTION AND ECOLOGY** India, Bangladesh, Myanmar, Thailand, Indo-China, Peninsular Malaysia, W and C Indonesia, to Sulawesi and the Philippines. Deciduous and evergreen lowland forests to 800m elevation. **USES** Timber hard and durable. Often planted as a street tree. Previously known as *Fagraea fragrans*.

Limahlania crenulata
■ *Cabbage Tree* (*Malabera, Berah*)

DESCRIPTION Evergreen or partly deciduous tree to 20m tall, with distinctive pagoda-shaped crown and open, horizontal branching. Trunk armed with sharp prickles when young. Leaves 18–40cm long, opposite, broadly obovate. Flowers 3–4cm long, funnel shaped, creamy-yellow, in dense terminal clusters. Fruits 2–3cm long, ellipsoid, dull green.

DISTRIBUTION AND ECOLOGY Vietnam, Thailand, Peninsular Malaysia, Sumatra and Borneo. Open, swampy ground near coasts. **USES** Timber used for pilings. Sometimes planted as an ornamental. Known until recently as *Fagraea crenulata*.

Utania racemosa
■ *False Coffee Tree*

DESCRIPTION Evergreen shrub or small tree to 12m tall, with regular horizontal branching when young. Leaves 15–25cm long, opposite, elliptic-oblong to obovate. Flowers 2.5–3.5cm long in terminal spike-like clusters, corolla funnel shaped, creamy-white to pale orange or pinkish. Fruits *c.* 1.2cm long, ellipsoid, pale yellow.

DISTRIBUTION AND ECOLOGY SE Asia to N Australia and Solomon Islands. Semi-open areas at edges of evergreen forests or moist secondary forests at low elevations. **USES** Sometimes planted as an ornamental. Known until recently as *Fragraea racemosa*.

HAMAMELIDACEAE (WITCH-HAZELS)

Maingaya malayana
■ Malayan Witch Hazel

DESCRIPTION
Evergreen tree to
27m tall. Leaves
10–25cm long, elliptic
to lanceolate. Flowers
creamy-yellow, in dense
spherical heads 2–2.5cm
across. Fruits 1–1.5cm
long, fused in lumpy woody capsule. **DISTRIBUTION AND ECOLOGY** Genus with a single species, endemic in S Thailand and Peninsular Malaysia. Lowland to hill evergreen forests. **USES** Sometimes planted as an ornamental.

Rhodoleia championii
■ Hong Kong Rose (*Kerlik*)

DESCRIPTION Evergreen shrub or tree to 25m tall. Leaves 5–14cm long, ovate to elliptic-oblong. Flowers in spherical heads surrounded by whorl of 12–20 conspicuous pink to bright red bracts, 1.5–2.5cm across. Fruits in woody spherical heads 1.5–2.5cm across. **DISTRIBUTION AND ECOLOGY** S China, NE Myanmar, W Thailand, N Vietnam, Peninsular Malaysia and Sumatra. Evergreen forests at 600–1,000m altitude. **USES** Occasionally planted in parks or roadsides at higher altitudes in Java.

HYPERICACEAE
(ST JOHN'S WORTS)

Cratoxylum formosum
■ *Gerongang*

DESCRIPTION Deciduous tree to
45m tall, with open crown and slender
branches. Leaves 5–7cm long, opposite,
oval to elliptic-oblong. Flowers 1.5–2.5cm
long, white or pink, clustered along
leafless twigs or behind young leaves.
Fruits 1.2–1.8cm long, ellipsoid to
narrowly ovoid, with pointed tips.

DISTRIBUTION AND ECOLOGY
Andaman Islands, S Thailand, Cambodia,
S Vietnam, SE China, Peninsular
Malaysia, Sumatra, Java, Banka, Borneo,
Sulawesi and the Philippines. Semi-open
areas and secondary forests in lowlands.

USES Produces durable timber but not
harvested commercially. Occasionally
planted as an ornamental.

LAMIACEAE (MINTS)

Clerodendrum paniculatum
■ Pagoda Flower

DESCRIPTION Evergreen shrub to 1.5m tall. Leaves up to 30cm long, opposite, subcordate to orbicular to ovate, 3–5 lobes. Flowers in terminal pagoda-shaped clusters, 1.5cm wide, pink, orange-red or red. Fruits 0.5–1cm across, globose. **DISTRIBUTION AND ECOLOGY** S China and SE Asia. Lowland forests in disturbed habitats and on stream banks. **USES** Often planted as an ornamental for its attractive flowers. There is also a yellow-flowered form.

Clerodendrum quadriloculare ■ Starburst (Quezonia, Shooting Star)

DESCRIPTION Evergreen shrub to 5m tall. Leaves 15–20cm long, opposite or whorled, ovate to oblong, green on top, purple underneath. Flowers in large, showy terminal clusters with narrow pink tube to 7cm long. Fruit a drupe. **DISTRIBUTION AND ECOLOGY** Papua New Guinea and the Philippines. Can become invasive and has naturalized in many tropical countries. Secondary vegetation and disturbed habitats. **USES** Planted as an ornamental.

Gmelina elliptica ■ Common Bulang
(*Bulang, Pukang Mata Hari*)

DESCRIPTION Evergreen straggly shrub or small tree to 6m tall, with woody thorns. Leaves 4–9cm long, covered with densely white, felt-like hairs below, ovate to lanceolate. Flowers 2–4cm long, yellow. Fruits *c*. 1.8cm long, spherical to obovoid.
DISTRIBUTION AND ECOLOGY Andaman and Nicobar Islands, and SE Asia excluding New Guinea. Scrubby areas, especially on sandy soil near the sea.
USES Sometimes used in traditional medicine for headaches and swellings.

Tectona grandis ■ Teak (*Jati*)

DESCRIPTION Large deciduous tree to 30m tall, with rather narrow, irregular crown. Leaves 15–60cm long, opposite, broadly obovate to oval. Flowers *c*. 0.7cm long, white, sometimes with pinkish tinge, in terminal widely branched, pyramidal clusters. Fruits 1.8–2.5cm long, dry, papery calyx enveloping hairy stone, *c*. 1cm, with 4 cavities each containing 1 seed.
DISTRIBUTION AND ECOLOGY India, Myanmar, N Thailand, Cambodia, Laos and Vietnam. Lowland deciduous forests.
USES Widely planted for its timber. Produces one of the most prized timbers in SE Asia.

Teijsmanniodendron pteropodum

DESCRIPTION Evergreen tree to 24m tall, with spreading crown. Leaves digitate with 5–7 unequal leaflets, opposite, 10–30cm long, elliptic-oblong to obovate, petiole winged. Flowers *c*. 1.2cm long, in open, branched terminal cluster, lilac to purple. Fruits 2.5–4cm long, ovoid with many faint ridges.

DISTRIBUTION AND ECOLOGY India, Nicobar Islands, S Thailand, Peninsular Malaysia, Singapore, Sumatra, Borneo and the Philippines. Lowland evergreen forests. **USES** Timber is durable and used for rafters, interior work, boxes and crates. Attractive foliage, and has potential as an ornamental tree.

Vitex negundo ■ Chinese Chaste Tree
(Five-leaved Chaste Tree, Horseshoe Vitex)

DESCRIPTION Shrub or small, bushy tree to 8m tall. Leaves digitate with 3–5 leaflets, opposite, central one 6–12cm long, narrowly elliptic to lanceolate, usually distinctly toothed. Flowers *c*. 0.7cm long, pale blue to deep purple in terminal spike-like cluster, stalk purple. Fruits 0.4–0.8cm long, oval to about globose. **DISTRIBUTION AND ECOLOGY** E Africa, India and S China. Secondary growth and wasteland. Commonly planted in SE Asia, and possibly not native. **USES** Widely used as a folk medicine.

Vitex pinnata
■ Malayan Teak (*Leban*)

DESCRIPTION Evergreen tree to 24m tall. Leaves digitate with 3–5 leaflets, rarely trifoliate, opposite, central leaflet 11–20cm long, ovate to elliptic. Flowers 1.2–1.5cm long, white with blue or violet markings, sometimes yellow or pinkish, in untidy terminal branched clusters. Fruits *c.* 0.8cm across, spherical, green ripening glossy purple to black. **DISTRIBUTION AND ECOLOGY** India, Sri Lanka and SE Asia. Secondary growth. **USES** Timber from older and more mature trees is durable and hard.

LAURACEAE (LAURELS)

Cinnamomum iners
■ Wild Cinnamon (*Medang Teja, Kayu Manis Hutan*)

DESCRIPTION Evergreen tree to 24m tall, with rounded or cylindrical, bushy crown. Leaves opposite or sub-opposite, 7.5–30cm long, elliptic, trinerved; young leaves have attractive pink flush, turning yellow and subsequently green. Flowers creamy in terminal and axillary clusters. Fruits oblong, *c.* 1.5cm long.

DISTRIBUTION AND ECOLOGY India, Myanmar, Thailand, Indo-China, Peninsular Malaysia, Sumatra, Borneo and the Philippines. Common in lowland and hill forests, including secondary forests. **USES** Often planted as a shade tree. Wood used in manufacture of fragrant joss sticks.

Cinnamomum porrectum
■ Safrol Laurel (*Medang Kemangi*)

DESCRIPTION Evergreen tree to 45m tall, with spreading crown. Leaves spirally arranged to sub-opposite, penninerved, whitish waxy below, 5–15cm long, elliptic or ovate. Flowers

pale yellow, sweet scented, in axillary and pseudoterminal clusters. Fruits globose, 0.8cm across. **DISTRIBUTION AND ECOLOGY** India, S China and most of SE Asia. Widespread from coasts to mountain forests. **USES** Wood used for general construction.

Persea americana ■ Avocado

DESCRIPTION
Evergreen tree to
10m or more tall.
Leaves 8–20cm long,
narrowly elliptic.
Flowers 5–6mm across,
in branched clusters,
yellowish-green. Fruits
8–18cm long, yellow-
green or reddish-brown, usually pear shaped,
sometimes ovoid or globose; mesocarp fleshy
and edible. **DISTRIBUTION AND ECOLOGY**
Mexico. Humid lowland forests on limestone
formations. **USES** Fruit is widely appreciated, with a buttery textured flesh. It is eaten raw
or made into drinks. Tree is extensively cultivated in tropical and subtropical regions.

LECYTHIDACEAE (BRAZIL NUT AND CANNONBALL TREE)

Barringtonia acutangula ■ Stream Barringtonia (Red Barringtonia, *Putat Sawa*)

DESCRIPTION Small evergreen tree to 13m
tall. Leaves 6–20cm long, narrowly obovate,
margin finely toothed. Flowers 1.5–2.5cm
across, in dense, slender pendulous raceme,
pink or red; stamens deep pink or dark red.
Flowers open nocturnally and by morning
they begin to drop. Fruits 2–6cm across,
ellipsoid or ovoid or globose with 4–8 ribs,
brownish and scurfy.

**DISTRIBUTION
AND ECOLOGY**
Afghanistan, Indian
subcontinent, Indo-
China, the Philippines,
Malaysia, Indonesia,
Papua New Guinea
and N Australia.
Common along streams
and in understorey of
lowland forests. **USES**
Sometimes planted as
an ornamental.

Barringtonia asiatica

■ Beach Barringtonia (Sea Putat, *Putat Laut*)

DESCRIPTION Evergreen tree 7–20m tall. Leaves 15–52cm long, obovate, entire margin. Flowers *c.* 5–8cm across, in terminal raceme, erect, white; stamens white at base, pink or red distally. Flowers open nocturnally and by morning they begin to drop. Fruits ovoid, tetragonous, 8.5–10cm across. **DISTRIBUTION AND ECOLOGY** Very widespread species, common along coasts of Indian Ocean into SE Asia, Australia and Pacific islands. Littoral species of sandy seashores. **USES** Planted as an ornamental.

Barringtonia racemosa

■ Common Putat (Powder-puff Tree, *Putat Ayam*)

DESCRIPTION Small to medium-sized tree to 20m tall. Leaves clustered at tips of branches, 14–42cm long, obovate-oblong, margin serrated. Flowers in terminal racemes arising from mature branches, white, sometimes tinged pink, 1.5–2.5cm long, with white, purple or red stamens. Flowers open nocturnally and by morning they begin to drop. Fruits ellipsoid, 5–9cm long. **DISTRIBUTION AND ECOLOGY** Very widespread species: E and S Africa, Comoros, Madagascar, Seychelles, India, Sri Lanka, Andaman Islands, Nicobar Islands, Myanmar, Thailand, China, throughout SE Asia, to Australia and Pacific islands. Common in primary and secondary lowland forests, mostly in periodically inundated forests or swampy places, along lakes and seashores; occasionally in hill forests. **USES** Planted as an ornamental.

Couroupita guianensis ■ Cannonball Tree

DESCRIPTION Medium-sized deciduous tree to 35m tall. Leaves clustered at tips of branches, 8–31cm long, obovate to elliptic. Flowers borne on racemes to 80cm long, from main trunk, 6cm across, pink to red. Fruits spherical, with brown woody shell reaching diameter of up to 25cm. **DISTRIBUTION AND ECOLOGY** Native in rainforests of C and S America. **USES** Widely cultivated for its beautiful flowers and interesting fruits.

Gustavia superba
■ Heaven Lotus (*Membrillo*)

DESCRIPTION Small tree to 15m tall. Leaves up to 100cm long, elliptic-oblanceolate, coarsely toothed. Flowers to 12cm across, white. Fruits depressed-globose, 7–10cm across, pale yellow to orange at maturity. **DISTRIBUTION AND ECOLOGY** Costa Rica to Colombia. Lowland tropical moist forests. **USES** Cultivated as an ornamental for its attractive large flowers.

Lecythis ollaria ▪ Monkey Pot (Paradise Nut, Sapucaia)

DESCRIPTION Medium-sized evergreen tree to 35m tall. Leaves 6–15cm long, elliptic to ovate. Flowers in terminal unbranched clusters, 5–8cm across, white with tinge of purple. Fruits 20–26cm across, woody, cup or pot shaped, brown, capsule with thick pericarp. Seeds oval, with many ridges and grooves on surface. **DISTRIBUTION AND ECOLOGY** Venezuela and Brazil. Lowland forests and river valleys. **USES** Nuts are edible, said to be better tasting than Brazil nuts. The nuts, however, can be toxic when they come from trees growing in selenium-rich soils as the species accumulates selenium.

LYTHRACEAE (LOOSESTRIFES)

Duabanga grandiflora ▪ Duabanga (*Beremban Bukit*)

DESCRIPTION Evergreen tree to 40m tall, with straight bole and whorls of horizontal side branches when young. Leaves opposite, 10–27cm long, narrowly ovate to oblong-lanceolate. Flowers 6–8cm across, in terminal branched clusters, white. Fruits 2.7–4.5cm across, broadly ovate, seated on large, woody, star-shaped calyx. **DISTRIBUTION AND ECOLOGY** N India, Andaman Islands, S China, Myanmar, Thailand, Cambodia, Laos, Vietnam and Peninsular Malaysia. Frequent in secondary growth at lower altitudes. **USES** Timber not durable and used for boxes, planks and other general-purpose products. Young fruits are very sour and are sometimes eaten.

Lagerstroemia floribunda
■ Malayan Crepe Myrtle (Thai Crepe Myrtle, Kedah Bungur)

DESCRIPTION Partially deciduous or evergreen tree to 18m tall, with dense, bushy crown and crooked trunk. Leaves 10–22cm long, opposite, elliptic-oblong; young leaves pinkish to reddish-brown. Flowers *c.* 4cm across, pale pink or purple fading to white, in narrow terminal clusters of 20–40 flowers. Fruits 1.2–1.6cm long, capsule dark brown, oblong. **DISTRIBUTION AND ECOLOGY** Myanmar, Thailand, Cambodia, Laos, Vietnam and Peninsular Malaysia. Open riverbanks or limestone hills at low altitude. **USES** Popular as an ornamental; a reddish-leaved form is now widely planted in Malaysia

Lagerstroemia indica ■ Crepe Myrtle

DESCRIPTION Shrub or small evergreen or deciduous bushy tree to 8m tall. Leaves 4–8cm long, opposite, oval to oblong, to obovate. Flowers 3.5–5cm across, pink to pale purple, or white. Fruits 1–1.3cm long, spherical, with persistent funnel-shaped calyx cup. **DISTRIBUTION AND ECOLOGY** Himalayas, China, Japan and Indo-China. Open, grassy places, forest edges and cliffs. **USES** Widely planted as an ornamental bush for its attractive flowers.

Lagerstroemia loudonii ■ Salao

DESCRIPTION Deciduous tree to 20m tall, with rounded crown and fluted trunk. Leaves 10–20cm long, opposite, elliptic-oblong; young leaves hairy below, soon losing the hairs. Flowers *c.* 5cm across, pink-purple fading to pale pink, mostly flowering in March–April when tree is leafless, in dense clusters on short side branches. Fruits 1.3–3cm long, spherical or oval, capsular. **DISTRIBUTION AND ECOLOGY** Endemic in NE Thailand. Dry deciduous forests. **USES** Cultivated as an ornamental for its spectacular blooms.

Lagerstroemia speciosa

■ Pride of India (Rose of India, Queen's Crepe Myrtle, *Bungor*)

DESCRIPTION Medium-sized deciduous tree to 25m tall, with dense, rounded crown. Leaves 12–18cm long, opposite, elliptic-oblong. Flowers 5–7cm across, very showy, bright pink to purple, in branched clusters. Fruits 1.8–2.5cm long, capsule oval or about globose, seated on calyx with 6 recurved lobes. **DISTRIBUTION AND ECOLOGY** India, Bangladesh, S China, Myanmar, Thailand, Cambodia, Laos, Vietnam, Peninsular Malaysia, Sumatra, Java, Borneo, Sulawesi, Lesser Sunda Island, Moluccas, the Philippines and W New Guinea. Frequent in seasonally flooded areas along streams or on bases of limestone hills. **USES** Widely cultivated as an ornamental tree. Wood produces high-quality timber.

Lawsonia inermis ■ Henna (*Inai*)

DESCRIPTION Shrub or small, straggly tree 2–6m tall, unarmed when young and often with spine-tipped twigs when older. Leaves 1.8–4cm long, opposite, elliptic to lanceolate. Flowers *c*. 1cm across, white to pale yellow turning red the following day, fragrant, in large, pyramidal branched clusters at ends of twigs. Fruits 4–8mm across, spherical, with persistent style at top and shallow calyx at base. **DISTRIBUTION AND ECOLOGY** India. Often naturalized in SE Asia. Dry coastal scrub wasteland to inland secondary vegetation. **USES** Widely cultivated for its fragrant flowers. Produces a well-known dye from leaves.

MAGNOLIACEAE (MAGNOLIAS)

Magnolia champaca ■ Yellow Champaca (*Champaca*)

DESCRIPTION Evergreen tree to 40m tall, with bushy crown. Leaves 10–20cm long, narrowly ovate. Flowers 4–5cm long, cream to creamy-yellow to orange, fragrant, solitary in leaf axils, facing upwards. Fruits loosely arranged in pendulous spiral cluster 6–30cm long, dehiscent, exposing seeds covered with reddish arils. **DISTRIBUTION AND ECOLOGY** India, Nepal, SW China, Myanmar, Thailand and Indo-China. Lowland forests. **USES** Cultivated for its fragrant flowers and as an ornamental tree. Timber durable and easy to work.

Magnolia x alba ■ White Champaca

DESCRIPTION Evergreen tree to 25m tall, with bushy crown. Leaves 19–40cm long, elliptic-oblong to oblanceolate. Flowers 5–6cm long, white to cream, in leaf axils, in pairs, flowering one at a time, facing upwards. Fruits similar to those of *M. champaca* (see p. 97), but more often the tree remains sterile. **DISTRIBUTION AND ECOLOGY** Probably a hybrid between *M. champaca* and *M. montana*, originating in Java and widely cultivated in S and SE Asia. **USES** As an ornamental tree and for its fragrant flowers.

Malpighiaceae

Lophanthera lactescens ■ Golden Chain Tree

DESCRIPTION Semi-deciduous tree 10–20m tall, with dense pyramidal crown. Leaves 20–25cm long, opposite or in whorls, obovate. Flowers *c.* 1cm long, yellow, clustered on long, pendulous raceme up to 40cm long. Fruits 2cm long. **DISTRIBUTION AND ECOLOGY** N Brazil. Amazon rainforest in open and secondary formations, usually on land not subjected to inundation. **USES** Often planted as an ornamental.

MALVACEAE (MALLOWS)

Abroma augusta ■ Devil's Cotton (*Ulat Kambai*)

DESCRIPTION Shrub to small tree to 10m tall. Leaves simple, 8–28cm long, heart shaped with trinerved bases. Flowers solitary, pendulous, dark red or purple with whitish bases, 1.5–2.5cm long. Fruit tops shaped with 5 deep ridges, splitting with long, irritant hairs along margins, 2.5–3cm long.
DISTRIBUTION AND ECOLOGY
Widespread in NE India, Bangladesh, S China, Thailand, Indo-China, Malaysia, Indonesia, the Philippines and N Australia. Scattered distribution in lowland evergreen forests. **USES** Silky fibres from bark are very strong and used to make cordage and fishing nets.

Ceiba pentandra ■ Silk Cotton Tree (Silk Cotton, *Kapuk*, *Kabu-kabu*)

DESCRIPTION Deciduous tree to 30m tall, with regular horizontal tiers of branches eventually forming spreading crown. Leaves digitate with 5–8 unequal leaflets 6–20cm long. Flowers 2.5–3.5cm long, creamy-white, in clusters. Fruits 8–15cm long, hanging in branches, ellipsoid, thinly woody, green maturing black, eventually splitting into 6 sections, exposing black kidney-shaped seeds embedded in dense mass of silky fibres.
DISTRIBUTION AND ECOLOGY W Africa and tropical America. Moist evergreen and deciduous forests. **USES** Commonly cultivated in villages for its cotton-like fibres, which are used to fill mattresses and pillows.

Commersonia bartramia ■
Scrub Christmas Tree (Brown Kurrajong)

DESCRIPTION Shrub or small tree to 12m tall, with spreading crown and horizontal branches. Leaves 8–20cm long, broadly ovate to ovate-oblong, often asymmetric, finely toothed all along margin. Flowers *c*. 0.8cm across, white or cream, bisexual, in branched clusters. Fruits 2–3cm across, completely covered with long bristles, pale green ripening pale brown, splitting into 5 sections, with 1–2 tiny, wingless seeds per section. **DISTRIBUTION AND ECOLOGY** S China, Vietnam, Thailand, Peninsular Malaysia, Borneo, the Philippines and Indonesia, to New Guinea, Solomon Islands and N Australia. Secondary growth and along roadsides.

Durio zibethinus ■ Durian

DESCRIPTION Evergreen tree to 30m tall. Leaves 10–18cm long, narrowly elliptic-oblong to lanceolate. Flowers along large branches, white or cream, 5–6cm long, fragrant; they open mainly at night, and are pollinated by bats. Fruits 20–40cm long, ovoid to ellipsoid, densely covered with broad pyramidal spines,

grey-green to yellowish, falling as intact fruits and each splitting into 5 segments on the ground. Seeds completely covered with strongly pungent flesh or yellowish edible aril. **DISTRIBUTION AND ECOLOGY** Not known in the wild; probably originates from Sumatra or Borneo. **USES** Widely cultivated for edible fruits.

Firmiana malayana
■ Bullock's Eye (*Mata Lembu*)

DESCRIPTION Deciduous tree to 28m tall, with narrow crown. Leaves broadly elliptic, occasionally 3 lobed, 10–20cm long. Flowers after complete leaf fall with whole crown completely covered in blossoms, in clusters at ends of shoots; calyx tube bright orange-red, and no corolla. Fruits 7.5–10cm long, in bunches on bare twigs, pale brownish, papery. **DISTRIBUTION AND ECOLOGY** Thailand, Peninsular Malaysia, Sumatra, Java and Borneo. Lowland forests and often near riverbanks. **USES** Sometimes planted as an ornamental.

Helicteres isora ■ Indian Screw Tree (*Cabai Pintal*)

DESCRIPTION Small tree or large shrub to 8m tall. Leaves ovate with serrated margins. Asymmetric flowers in small clusters in axils of branches; flowers characteristically change colour from bluish-grey on day one to light red on day two and dark red on day three, *c.* 4cm across. Pollinated by bees and birds. Fruits greenish ripening to brown or grey, compound capsule, twisted like a screw with a pointed end, *c.* 2cm long. **DISTRIBUTION AND ECOLOGY** Native on Indian subcontinent to SE Asia, S China and N Australia. Open areas in deciduous forests. **USES** Reported to have many medicinal uses.

Hibiscus mutabilis ■ Cotton Rose
(Confederate Rose, Rose of Sharon, Changeable Rose)

DESCRIPTION
Erect, robust deciduous or evergreen shrub or small tree, 1.5–5m tall. Leaves 10–15cm long, broadly ovate to round-ovate or cordate, 5–7 lobed. Flowers *c.* 12–15cm across, solitary, axillary on upper branches; petals white, turning red the day after opening or on the same afternoon in warmer climates. Fruits flattened globose capsule, *c.* 2.5cm diameter. **DISTRIBUTION AND ECOLOGY** S China and Taiwan. Forms thickets along streams. Occasionally naturalized in many countries. **USES** Widely cultivated as an ornamental. Cultivars with double petals have been called *H.mutabilis* f. *plenus.*

Hibiscus tiliaceus ■ Sea Hibiscus
(Beach Hibiscus, Cotton Tree, *Baru Baru, Bebaru*)

DESCRIPTION Shrubby evergreen tree to 15m tall. Leaves circular with heart-shaped bases, 8–15cm long. Flowers bright yellow with dark red-purple eye in the morning, fading to orange-pink in the afternoon and falling off on the same day, 7–9cm long. Fruits globose

to obovoid with persistent hairy calyx at base, drying and splitting open into 10 parts when ripe. **DISTRIBUTION AND ECOLOGY** Widely distributed throughout the tropics. Common on rocky or sandy coasts, and brackish rivers. **USES** Often planted as an ornamental.

Kleinhovia hospita
■ Guest Tree (Bataria Teak, *Temahai, Laban*)

DESCRIPTION Small evergreen tree to 12m tall, sometimes much taller. Leaves 8–15cm long, ovate to heart shaped. Flowers pink, 1.2–1.5cm long, in large terminal bunches. Fruits 2–3cm long, globose, deeply 5 lobed, bladder-like with inflated thin, papery wall, pale pink to brownish.

DISTRIBUTION AND ECOLOGY Widespread in W Africa, India, Sri Lanka, S China, Taiwan, Thailand, Peninsular Malaysia, Indonesia, the Philippines, Australia and Polynesia. Scattered but locally common in secondary forests, often near limestone hill bases. **USES** Sometimes planted as an ornamental.

Microcos tomentosa ■ *Chenderai*

DESCRIPTION Small, bushy tree to 15m tall, with dense, rounded or cylindrical crown. Leaves 8–20cm long, oblong to obovate, usually finely toothed at least on upper parts. Flowers *c.* 1.5cm long, pale yellow, in terminal clusters. Fruits 1–1.5cm long, globose to ellipsoid, bright green, ripening pale orange to blackish. **DISTRIBUTION AND ECOLOGY** Widespread species, native in E India, S China, Myanmar, Thailand, Indo-China, Peninsular Malaysia, Singapore, Sumatra, Java, Borneo and the Philippines. Very common in secondary forests, and forest edges of lowland evergreen and deciduous forests.

Schoutenia accrescens ■ *Bayur Bukit*

DESCRIPTION Deciduous tree to 30m tall, with coppery crown and slender, fluted trunk. Leaves 4–11cm long, small, lanceolate, slightly asymmetric, with dense, coppery stellate hairs beneath. Flowers 2.5–4cm across, in few-flowered clusters, only calyx, papery, broadly bell shaped, cream to pale yellow. Fruits 3–5cm long with persistent papery pale brown calyx surrounding a spherical nut *c*. 8mm in diameter. **DISTRIBUTION AND ECOLOGY** India, Sri Lanka, Thailand and Peninsular Malaysia. Widespread in lowland forests. **USES** Timber hard and durable. Not much planted as an ornamental but has good potential as one.

Sterculia cordata ■ *Kelumpang*

DESCRIPTION Deciduous tree to 20m tall. Leaves 12–24cm long, clustered towards ends of twigs, oblong-elliptic to obovate with cordate base, young shoots densely covered with soft hairs. Flowers unisexual, *c*. 0.5cm across, in lax, pendulous clusters 8–30cm long, pink to reddish-brown. Fruits 5–12cm long in groups of 2–3(–5) on pendulous common stalk, oblong-obovoid, leathery, densely yellow-brown hairy. **DISTRIBUTION AND ECOLOGY** Thailand, Peninsular Malaysia, Sumatra, Java and Borneo. Scattered in lowland forests. **USES** Sometimes planted as an ornamental.

Sterculia foetida ■ Hazel Sterculia

(Indian Almond, Java Olive, Skunk Tree, *Kalupat*, *Kabu-kabu*, *Kelumpang Jari*)

DESCRIPTION Large deciduous tree to 36m tall, with big, dome-shaped crown. Leaves digitate with 5–9 leaflets, 10–15cm long. Flowers unisexual, 2–2.5cm across, dark red, foul smelling, in loose, branched, drooping clusters. Fruits 8–12cm long in star-like clusters of 3–5 on long common stalk behind leaves, green maturing brick-red, dehiscing to expose bluish-black seeds. **DISTRIBUTION AND ECOLOGY** Widespread from E Africa, to most of tropical Asia, to N Australia. Common along rocky coasts and riverbanks. **USES** Widely planted as a street tree.

Sterculia macrophylla ■
Broad-leaved Sterculia (*Kelumpang Melian*)

DESCRIPTION Deciduous tree to 35m tall, sometimes taller, with straight trunk and clearly tiered whorls of branches. Leaves deeply heart shaped, 16–30cm long, clustered towards ends of branches. Flowers unisexual, *c.* 0.6cm across, in much-branched clusters of 20–40cm long, pale greenish-yellow with dull red or purple-brown hairs. Fruits 4–6.5cm long, in clusters of 3–5, spreading, globose to ellipsoid or obovoid, with blunt or rounded tips, ripening bright red, thickly leathery, and dehiscing to expose purple-black ellipsoid seeds. **DISTRIBUTION AND ECOLOGY** Thailand, Peninsular Malaysia, Sumatra, Java, Borneo, the Philippines and New Guinea. Infrequent in lowland forests, including freshwater swamp forests. **USES** Sometimes grown as an ornamental, and exploited for timber.

Sterculia megistophylla ■ *Kelumpang* (*Buah Anyantu, Sebayan, Beris Merah*)

DESCRIPTION Deciduous tree to 20m tall. Leaves 20–45cm long, narrowly elliptic, ovate to oblong-ovate. Flowers axillary or cauliflorous racemes, unisexual, brown-pink in bud, *c.* 2.5cm long. Fruits cauliflorous on main trunk in clusters of up to 5 bright red, leathery to woody follicles, 11–22cm long. Seeds ellipsoid, ripening black. Fruits large and very spectacular, hanging from trunk. **DISTRIBUTION AND ECOLOGY** Sumatra, Peninsular Malaysia and Borneo. Lowland forests. **USES** Makes an unusual ornamental tree, with its spectacular large red fruits hanging from the trunk.

Sterculia parviflora ■
Common Sterculia (*Kelumpang Burung, Samrong*)

DESCRIPTION Deciduous tree to 30m tall. Leaves 10–25cm long, elliptic-oblong with heart-shaped bases. Flowers unisexual, 0.8–1.2cm long, pale yellow with pink bases at first, becoming pink or red, in clusters behind leaf flushes. Fruits 7–12cm long, in groups of 4–5 on common stalk, ripening to bright orange-red, leathery with velvety hairs, with glossy black seeds.

DISTRIBUTION AND ECOLOGY Widespread in NE India, Myanmar, Thailand, Vietnam, Peninsular Malaysia, Singapore and N Borneo. Lowland forests. **USES** Occasionally planted as an ornamental.

Thespesia populnea ■ Bendy Tree
(Milo, Bhendi Tree, Portia Tree, Pacific Rosewood, *Bebaru*)

DESCRIPTION Evergreen tree to 15m tall, with spreading crown. Leaves 8–20cm long, heart shaped. Flowers solitary, *c*. 8cm long, pale yellow with red-purple centres in the morning, fading to dull reddish-pink in the late afternoon, and remaining on the tree for several days. Fruits 2.2–3.5cm long, spherical or slightly flattened on top.

DISTRIBUTION AND ECOLOGY Widely distributed along sea coasts throughout the tropics. Common along sandy and rocky coasts. **USES** Occasionally planted as an ornamental.

Meliaceae (Mahogany and Neem)

Aglaia macrocarpa ▪ *Bekak*

DESCRIPTION Large evergreen tree to 35m tall. Leaves to 70cm long, pinnately compound with terminal leaflets, 5–7 leaflets on each side of stalk. Flowers small, *c.* 1.6mm long, cream, in branched clusters *c.* 30cm long. Fruits capsular, 6–7.5cm long, bright red, dehiscing into 3 lobes when ripe.
DISTRIBUTION AND ECOLOGY Vietnam, Sumatra, Peninsular Malaysia, Borneo, the Philippines, Java, Sulawesi and Moluccas. Lowland and hill forests to 1,500m.

Azadirachta excelsa
▪ Gaint Neem Tree (*Sentang*)

DESCRIPTION Large evergreen tree to 50m tall. Leaves 20–60cm long, clustered at ends of twigs, pinnately compound without a terminal leaflet, 7–11 leaflets on each side of stalk. Flowers in erect long clusters, white, sweetly scented. Fruits 2.4–3.2cm long, ellipsoid, green ripening yellowish.
DISTRIBUTION AND ECOLOGY Vietnam, Peninsular Malaysia, Borneo, the Philippines, Sulawesi, Maluku and Irian Jaya. Rainforests at altitudes to 350m. **USES** Timber is considered to be one of the most attractive furniture timbers. Also used in house building and as a general utility timber. Grown on small-scale plantations.

Azadirachta indica ■ Neem (Indian Lilac)

DESCRIPTION Medium-sized evergreen to semi-deciduous tree 15–20m tall, with dense, rounded crown. Leaves 20–40cm long, pinnately compound with terminal leaflets, 10–15 leaflets on each side of rachis. Flowers 5–6mm across, white, fragrant, in loose clusters. Fruits 1.4–2.8cm long, ellipsoid, yellowish. **DISTRIBUTION AND ECOLOGY** Indian subcontinent. Tropical and semi-tropical forests. **USES** Widely used as a traditional medicine. Young leaves and flowers eaten as a vegetable in India. Often grown as an ornamental.

Khaya senegalensis ■ Dry Zone Mahogany
(Senegal Mahogany, African Mahogany, Senegal Khaya, *Bisselon*)

DESCRIPTION Large evergreen or sometimes deciduous tree in drier climates, to 30m tall, with large, rounded crown. Leaves up to 25cm long, pinnately compound without a terminal leaflet, 3–6 leaflets on each side of rachis. Flowers small, *c*. 1cm across, cream to white, in branched clusters to 20cm long. Fruits 4–6cm across, globose, woody capsule dehiscing into 4 valves when ripe. **DISTRIBUTION AND ECOLOGY** Senegal to Sudan and Uganda. Riverine forests and higher rainfall savannah woodland. **USES** Important timber tree, highly valued for furniture and construction. Heartwood an attractive dark red-brown timber, often with a purple tint. Widely planted as a street tree in SE Asia.

Lansium domesticum ▪ Langsat (*Duku, Duku-langsat, Dokong*)

DESCRIPTION Medium-sized evergreen tree to 30m tall. Leaves 30–50cm long, pinnately compound, without a terminal leaflet, 2–4 leaflets on each side of rachis. Flowers small, *c*. 2–3mm long, scented, creamy-white, clustered in racemes on main trunk and branches. Fruits 2–4cm long, ellipsoid, ripening yellowish-brown, with fleshy arils. **DISTRIBUTION AND ECOLOGY** Peninsular Thailand, Peninsular Malaysia, Sumatra, Java, Borneo, the Philippines, Sulawesi, Moluccas and Iran Jaya. Lowland evergreen forests. **USES** Widely cultivated for its edible fruits. Wild plants have very sour fruits. Different cultivars are known locally by names such as *Duku, Duku-langsat* and *Dokong*.

Melia azedarach ▪ Chinaberry (Pride of India, Cape Lilac)

DESCRIPTION Medium-sized deciduous tree 20–45m tall. Leaves 20–40cm long, bipinnate or occasionally tripinnate, 3–11 leaflets on each side of rachis, serrated. Flowers showy, 1cm long, lilac, in axillary branched clusters. Fruits *c*. 1–2cm across, ovoid to globose, yellowish-brown. **DISTRIBUTION AND ECOLOGY** India, Sri Lanka, Nepal, Bangladesh, Myanmar, Thailand, Indo-China, S China, S Japan and Irian Jaya. Deciduous lowland forests. **USES** Planted as an ornamental, as a windbreak. Leaves sometimes used in traditional medicine.

Sandoricum koetjape

■ Cotton Fruit (*Sentul*)

DESCRIPTION Large tree to 45m tall, with thick, rounded crown. Leaves 18–40cm long, trifoliate. Flowers small, *c*. 5mm across, yellow-green to white, in branched clusters. Fruits 5–8cm across, globose to subglobose, ripening yellowish-brown to pale brown. **DISTRIBUTION AND ECOLOGY** Widely planted in tropical Asia, but wild form probably extends from Peninsular Malaysia and Sumatra to New Guinea. Lowland evergreen forests. **USES** Planted widely for its edible fruits, eaten both fresh and cooked.

Walsura pinnata

DESCRIPTION Medium-sized tree 12–37m tall. Leaves to 50cm long, pinnately compound with terminal leaflets, 2–3 leaflets on each side of rachis. Flowers small, *c*. 3mm across, white to pale yellow, in branched clusters. Fruits 1.2–2.5cm long, spherical to ovoid, ripening brownish golden-yellow. **DISTRIBUTION AND ECOLOGY** S China, Vietnam, Myanmar, Thailand, Peninsular Malaysia, Java, Borneo, the Philippines, Moluccas and Irian Jaya. Lowland to hill forests.

MORACEAE (MULBERRIES OR FIGS)

Antiaris toxicaria
■ Ipoh Tree (Upas Tree, Sacking Tree)

DESCRIPTION Large deciduous, monoecious (having male and female flowers on the same tree) tree to 40m tall, with spreading crown. Leaves elliptic to obovate, 7–19cm long. Flower heads on leafy twigs. Male inflorescence boat-like, *c.* 1.5cm wide; female inflorescence pear shaped, single flowered. Fruit a drupe ripening red to purple-red, *c.* 2cm diameter. **DISTRIBUTION AND ECOLOGY** India, Sri Lanka, Myanmar, Thailand, Vietnam, S China, Malaysia, Indonesia, New Guinea and N Australia.

Lowland to lower montane forests. **USES** Latex of tree is poisonous and is used with the sap of *Strychnos* species in dart and arrow poison for hunting and warfare purposes. Timber sold as a light hardwood.

Artocarpus altilis ■ Breadfruit (*Sukun*)

DESCRIPTION Evergreen to deciduous, monoecious tree to 20m tall, with large, roundish crown. Leaves 30–60cm long, ovate to elliptic, deeply lobed. Flower heads on leafy twigs. Male flower head club shaped; female flower head stiffly upright. Fruits 12.5–30cm across, globose, smooth or prickly with stout stalks. **DISTRIBUTION AND ECOLOGY** Pacific islands. Cultivated throughout the tropics. **USES** Fruits edible and are the staple food for many cultures. Cooked fruits are like freshly baked bread and have a potato-like flavour.

Artocarpus elasticus ■ *Terap Nasi*

DESCRIPTION Evergreen monecious tree to 45m tall, with strong buttresses and roundish crown. Leaves 23–55cm long, rough hairy on upper surface and densely hairy on lower surface. Flower heads on leafy twigs, Male flower head finger-like; female flower head upright, barrel shaped. Fruits cylindrical, *c.* 10–12cm long, yellow-brown with soft, recurved spines. **DISTRIBUTION AND ECOLOGY** Myanmar, Thailand, Peninsular Malaysia, Sumatra, Borneo, Java, Lesser Sunda Islands and the Philippines. Common in lowland forests and open secondary forests. The most common *Artocarpus* in secondary vegetation. **USES** Fruits edible but hardly ever eaten. Produces a light hardwood timber.

Artocarpus heterophyllus ■ Jackfruit (*Nangka*)

DESCRIPTION Evergreen monecious tree to 20m tall, with conical to rounded crown. Leaves 5–20cm long, elliptic to obovate. Male flower heads barrel shaped, 3.5–7.5cm long, on leafy twigs or on short fruiting twigs from the trunk; female flower heads on main trunk and on large branches. Fruits 30–100cm long, barrel or pear shaped, cream to golden-yellow, set with sharp conical warts. **DISTRIBUTION AND ECOLOGY** Probably native in S India. Widely cultivated in SE Asia for its edible fruits and seeds. **USES** Fruits eaten raw. Seeds sometimes roasted or boiled, and have a nutty flavour. Produces a light hardwood timber.

Artocarpus integer ■ *Chempedak*

DESCRIPTION Evergreen monecious tree to 24m tall, with conical to rounded crown. Twigs and leaves covered with long hairs. Leaves 8–20cm long, elliptic to oblong-elliptic. Male flower heads cylindrical, smaller than female's, on leafy twigs or on short fruiting twigs; female flower heads on main trunk. Fruits mostly on main trunk, cylindrical, up to 35cm long, yellow with sets of flat warts with a strong, harsh penetrating odour. **DISTRIBUTION AND ECOLOGY** Only known in cultivation and widely cultivated for its edible fruits and seeds in SE Asia. **USES** Fleshy fruits very often eaten fried in batter; seeds are also edible.

Artocarpus integer var. *silvestris*
■ *Bangkong*

DESCRIPTION Evergreen tree to 50m tall. Like cultivated variety except that it is less hairy and its fruits do not ripen

with a strong odour. **DISTRIBUTION AND ECOLOGY** Thailand, Peninsular Malaysia, Borneo, Sumatra, Java, Sulawesi and the Philippines. Lowland to hill evergreen forests. Only occurs in the wild. **USES** Young fruits and seeds sometimes collected for food. They are cooked very much like breadfruit.

Artocarpus rigidus ■ Monkey Jack
(Tempunai, Temponek)

DESCRIPTION Evergreen monecious tree to 45m tall. Leaves 6.5–26cm long, elliptic, obovate or rounded, very variable in size and shape. Flower heads in leaf axils. Male flower heads obovoid to globose, 1.2–2.5cm across. Fruits up to 15cm across, globose, greenish-yellow ripening dull orange, thickly set with stiff, conical spines.

DISTRIBUTION AND ECOLOGY Myanmar, Thailand, Indo-China, Peninsular Malaysia, Sumatra, Borneo and Java. Frequent in lowland and hill forests. **USES** Fruits edible. Produces a light hardwood timber.

Artocarpus scortechinii ■ *Terap Hitam*

DESCRIPTION Evergreen monecious tree to 35m tall with strong buttresses and roundish crown. Similar to *A. elasticus* (see p. 115) but leaves smaller, smooth and glabrous on upper surface, and soft densely hairy on lower surface. Flower heads on leafy twigs, male finger-like, female upright, ovoid. Fruits cylindrical, *c.* 10–12cm long, yellow-brown, not set with long soft spines.

DISTRIBUTION AND ECOLOGY Peninsular Malaysia and Lingga Islands, and Sumatra. Common in lowland forests and open secondary forest. **USES** Fruits edible but hardly eaten. Produces a light hardwood timber.

Ficus auriculata

■ Roxburgh's Fig (Broad-leaf Fig, Giant Indian Fig, Elephant Ear Fig, Himalayan Fig)

DESCRIPTION Small, spreading tree to 12m tall, with very large leaves and large reddish figs on short stalks growing from branches at base of trunk. Leaves 30cm long or more, heart shaped. Figs 5–9cm across, stalked, pear shaped, reddish-brown, edible, flesh red-purple. **DISTRIBUTION AND ECOLOGY** Himalayas, S China, Indo-China, Thailand and possibly wild in N Peninsular Malaysia. Lowland forests. **USES** Cultivated for its edible fruits.

Ficus benghalensis ■ Indian Banyan (Banyan Tree)

DESCRIPTION Large strangling fig to 20m tall. Spreading crown with abundant aerial roots, spreading to 100m or more. Aerial roots turn woody, forming pillar-like prop roots once reaching the ground. Leaves hairy, ovate to elliptic, 2–6cm long, coriaceous. Figs sessile, in axillary pairs, globose, 1.5–2cm diameter, ripening pinkish-red, hairy. **DISTRIBUTION AND ECOLOGY** Widespread in India, Pakistan and Bangladesh. Lowland forests. **USES** Fruits edible. Widely cultivated as an ornamental in the tropics and elsewhere.

Ficus hispida

DESCRIPTION Small evergreen tree to 12m tall. Twigs, leaves and figs set with short, rather bristly white hairs. Leaves 5.5–35cm long, generally opposite, oblong, margin faintly toothed. Figs on leafless hanging twigs from trunks and main branches, 2.5–3.8cm across, stalked, obovoid.

DISTRIBUTION AND ECOLOGY Widespread from India to Sri Lanka, S China, Peninsular Malaysia, Singapore, Sumatra, Java, Borneo, the Philippines, Sulawesi, New Guinea and Australia (Queensland). Common in secondary vegetation.

Ficus lyrata ■ Fiddle-leaf Fig (Lyre-leaf Fig)

DESCRIPTION Evergreen tree to 30m tall, often much shorter in cultivation. Crown dense and rounded. Leaves large, to 30cm long, obovate to lyre shaped, often with wavy margin, base cordate. Figs in axils of leaves near apex, sessile, globose, green with yellow spots, and hard, 3–5cm across. **DISTRIBUTION AND ECOLOGY** Native in lowland forests of tropical Africa. **USES** Widely cultivated as an ornamental. Tolerates shade as an indoor plant, but loses its lower leaves early in these conditions.

Ficus microcarpa ■ Malayan Banyan (*Jawi Jawi, Jejawi*)

DESCRIPTION Large strangler with numerous tassels of slender aerial roots from branches and twigs, some developing into pillar roots. Leaves blunt or scarcely pointed, often asymmetric. Figs sessile, ripening pink to dull purple, with 3 small yellow scales at base. **DISTRIBUTION AND ECOLOGY** India to Solomon Islands. Especially common in swampy habitats. **USES** Cultivated as an ornamental.

Ficus oligodon ■ Apple Fig

DESCRIPTION Small tree to 12m tall. Leaves 12.5–25cm long, elliptic or ovate with distinct trinerve base, coarsely toothed. Figs pear or apple shaped, 2.75–6.3cm across, green, ripening yellow to red with green spots; arranged in big clusters on trunk and main branches on

woody knobs or stout, woody, leafless twigs. **DISTRIBUTION AND ECOLOGY** Widespread in E Himalayas, Myanmar, Thailand, S China, Indo-China and N Peninsular Malaysia. Frequently found by streams and rivers in lowlands and mountains. **USES** Fruits edible.

Ficus racemosa ■ Red River Fig

DESCRIPTION Medium-sized or tall deciduous tree to 25m tall, without aerial roots. Leaves 6.5–15cm long, elliptic, distinctly toothed. Figs 3–5cm wide, pear shaped with short stalks, ripening rose-red, often streaked; arranged in big clusters on trunk and main branches and borne on stout, woody, leafless twigs.
DISTRIBUTION AND ECOLOGY SE Asia to Australia. Widespread by riverbanks in India.

Ficus superba ■ Sea Fig

DESCRIPTION Deciduous strangling tree to 30m tall, with spreading, lanky branches and few aerial roots. Leaves 8–24cm long on long, slender petioles, spirally arranged or clustered at ends of twigs, elliptic-oblong. Figs 1–1.5cm on slender stalks, globose to slightly pear shaped, ripening pink to dark maroon with whitish patches.
DISTRIBUTION AND ECOLOGY Vietnam, Cambodia, Thailand, Peninsular Malaysia and W Indonesia. Coastal areas on rocky boulders and in open areas.

Ficus variegata ■ Common Red Stem Fig

DESCRIPTION Medium-sized deciduous tree to 40m tall, with conical then rounded, dense crown. Leaves 9–25cm long, broadly ovate to ovate-lanceolate, with trinerved base. Figs 1.8–3.8cm long in dense clusters on trunk and main branches, on long stalks, pear shaped, green turning rose-red, often streaked. **DISTRIBUTION AND ECOLOGY** India, S China, whole of SE Asia except New Guinea, and Australia (Queensland). Common in open country.

MORINGACEAE

Moringa oleifera ■ Horse-radish Tree
(Drumstick Tree, *Kelur*, *Merunggai*)

DESCRIPTION Small deciduous tree 10–12m tall with umbrella-shaped open crown and sparse foliage. Leaves tripinnate compound, 30–60cm long, leaflets obovate. Flowers in clusters, fragrant, white or creamy white, 2.5cm across. Fruits pendulous pods, cylindrical, brown splitting into 3 parts on maturity. **DISTRIBUTION AND ECOLOGY** Native to India to Arabia, and possibly Africa and the East Indies. Dry subtropical to moist tropical forest. Widely planted in the tropics. **USES** A multi-purpose tree and almost every part is of value for food. Foliage is eaten as greens in both salads and vegetable curries. Fruits are also eaten, especially the immature fruits in curries. Oil is extracted from the mature seeds as edible oil and also used in arts, and for lubricating watches and other delicate machinery.

Muntingiaceae

Muntingia calabura

■ Calabura (Japanese Cherry, Malayan Cherry, Jamaican Cherry, Cherry Tree, *Buah Cheri*)

DESCRIPTION Small evergreen tree 3–12m tall, with fan-like branches. Leaves 4–14cm long, ovatelanceolate with serrated margin. Flowers white, 1.2–2cm wide, with many prominent stamens. Fruits 1–1.25cm across, globose, green ripening orangey-yellow, with soft pulp filled with tiny seeds. **DISTRIBUTION AND ECOLOGY** Tropical America. Widely grown as a village tree, and often naturalized. **USES** Fruits edible, and sometimes made into a jam.

Myristicaceae (Nutmegs)

Horsfieldia superba

DESCRIPTION Small to medium-sized evergreen tree to 28m tall, with columnar crown. Leaves 25–35cm long, elliptic to narrowly obovate. Flowers unisexual, with male and female flowers on different trees, *c.* 5–12mm across, in branched clusters, behind leaves; male flowers more branched than female flowers. Fruits *c.* 9cm long, ovoid, orange. **DISTRIBUTION AND ECOLOGY** Endemic in Peninsular Malaysia. Lowland forests.

Myristica fragrans
■ Nutmeg (*Pokok Pala*)

DESCRIPTION Small evergreen tree 3–13m tall, with columnar crown. Leaves 5–12cm long, elliptic to ovate. Flowers unisexual, with male and female flowers on different trees, small, *c.* 1mm across, covered with brown hairs. Fruits 6–9cm long, solitary, broadly pear shaped or almost globose, yellow to dull brown. **DISTRIBUTION AND ECOLOGY** Moluccas. Humid lowland forests. Widely grown across the tropics. **USES** Main source of the spices nutmeg and mace. Fleshy mesocarp is sometimes pickled in sugar to make sweets.

MYRTACEAE (MYRTLES)

Baeckea frutescens
■ False Ru (*Cucor Atap*)

DESCRIPTION Shrub or small evergreen tree to 5m tall, with pendent branches. Leaves opposite, needle-like, *c.* 1cm long. Flowers 3–4mm across, cream-pink, solitary, axillary. Fruits capsular, urn shaped, 3mm diameter, ripening reddish-brown. **DISTRIBUTION AND ECOLOGY** Widespread from S China to Thailand, Sumatra, Peninsular Malaysia, Borneo, Sulawesi, New Guinea and Australia. Mainly confined to vegetation on dry sandy or rocky coastal bluffs. **USES** Occasionally planted as an ornamental.

Leptospermum javanicum
■ Tea Tree (*Gelam Bukit*)

DESCRIPTION Evergreen shrub or small, gnarled tree to 8m tall, with flat-branched crown of twisted branches. Leaves 10–18mm long, obovate to oblanceolate. Flowers solitary, axillary, *c*. 14mm across, white. Fruits spherical, *c*. 5mm across, 5-valved capsule. **DISTRIBUTION AND ECOLOGY** Myanmar, S Thailand, Sumatra, Peninsular Malaysia, Borneo, Java, the Philippines and Sulawesi. On high mountains in rocky places in montane to upper montane forests. **USES** Occasionally planted as an ornamental.

Leptospermum madidum
■ Weeping Tea-tree

DESCRIPTION Shrub or small evergreen tree to 4m tall, with wide, spreading crown and thin, trailing branches. Leaves narrowly linear, 5–7cm long. Flowers solitary, axillary, 5mm across, white. Fruits urn shaped, 3–4mm across, woody, ripening dark brown before dehiscing to disperse seeds. **DISTRIBUTION AND ECOLOGY** Endemic in Northern Territory of Australia. Along watercourses in sandstone gorges. **USES** Widely planted as an ornamental.

Melaleuca cajuputi
■ Paper-bark Tree (Tea Tree, Cajeput, *Gelam*)

DESCRIPTION Small to medium-sized evergreen tree to 20m tall, with oblong crown. Leaves 6–18cm long, lanceolate to sickle shaped, with veins parallel to margins. Flowers *c.* 5mm long, arranged in threes along a spike, white. Fruits a 3-valved capsule, *c.* 3mm across.

DISTRIBUTION AND ECOLOGY Seasonal regions from S Asia and S China, to the Philippines and Moluccas. Gregarious on infertile soils with impeded drainage. **USES** Often planted as an ornamental. Sometimes planted for firewood, posts and piling.

Psidium guajava ■ Guava (*Jambu Batu*)

DESCRIPTION Small evergreen tree to c. 10m tall, much branched with crooked stems. Leaves 7–15cm long, opposite, elliptic. Flowers c. 2.5cm across, solitary, axillary, white. Fruits c. 4–12cm long, globose, ovoid or pear shaped, green ripening yellow. **DISTRIBUTION AND ECOLOGY** Colombia, Mexico, Peru and USA. In native habitats, found in open areas of savannah/shrub transitional zones. Widely cultivated in the tropics for its edible fruits, and often naturalized. **USES** Fruits edible, and ripe fruits often made into juice.

Rhodomyrtus tomentosa
■ Rose-myrtle (*Kemunting*)

DESCRIPTION Evergreen shrub or treelet to 5m tall. Leaves 2.5–9cm long, opposite, lanceolate to elliptic. Flowers in axillary clusters of 3, c. 1.7–2cm across, pink, white. Fruits ellipsoid with persistent calyx, c. 15mm long. **DISTRIBUTION AND ECOLOGY** S and SE Asia, to Australia and New Caledonia. Common on degraded land, on sandy soils and sandy seashores to 1,000m. **USES** Fruits edible and can be made into jams. Occasionally planted as an ornamental.

Syzygium aqueum

■ Watery Rose-Apple (*Jambu Air*, *Tambis*)

DESCRIPTION Small evergreen tree to 15m tall. Leaves 9–19cm long, opposite, ovate-lanceolate to broadly elliptic-obovate. Flowers 2.5–3.5cm across, in terminal or axillary clusters of 3–7, white. Fruits pear shaped, *c.* 4cm long, white or pink, shiny. **DISTRIBUTION AND ECOLOGY** Thailand, Malaysia and Indonesia. Lowland forests, and widely cultivated. **USES** Fruits edible, eaten fresh or preserved.

Syzygium borneense
■ Bullate Eugenia

DESCRIPTION Medium-sized tree to 30m tall. Leaves 5–13cm long, elliptic-obovate, opposite. Flowers c. 4mm across, white, clustered along leaf axils on branches or ends of branches. Fruits 0.4–0.8cm across, globose, white tinged red or pink.

DISTRIBUTION AND ECOLOGY Peninsular Malaysia, Borneo, the Philippines and Sulawesi. Lowland evergreen forests and freshwater swamp forests to 600m altitude.

Syzygium grande ■ Sea Apple Tree
(*Kelat Laut, Jemah, Kerian Ayer*)

DESCRIPTION Large evergreen tree to 30m tall, with rounded, bushy crown. Leaves 12–20cm long, elliptic-ovate, opposite. Flowers 2.5–3.8cm across, white, in dense terminal or axillary clusters. Fruits *c.* 4cm long, ellipsoid, remaining green when ripe. **DISTRIBUTION AND ECOLOGY** SE India, Myanmar, Thailand, Peninsular Malaysia, Singapore and Borneo. Forests on rocky seashores and sandy beaches. **USES** Frequently planted as a roadside tree.

Syzygium jambos ■ Rose-apple (Malabar Plum, *Jambu Air Mawar*)

DESCRIPTION Small evergreen tree to 10m tall, with dense, spreading, bushy crown. Leaves 9–26cm long, narrowly elliptic to lanceolate, opposite. Flowers 5–10cm across, large pom-pom shaped, white with yellow tinge, in terminal clusters. Fruits 2.5–5cm across, globose to ovoid, ripening white to pale yellow **DISTRIBUTION AND ECOLOGY** S China to SE Asia. Widely cultivated and naturalized in tropical countries. Along white-water rivers to *c.* 700m altitude. **USES** Fruits edible, with sweet, rose-scented flesh.

Syzygium malaccense ■ Malay Apple
(Pomerac, *Jambu Bol*)

DESCRIPTION Small to medium-sized evergreen tree to
25m tall, with columnar dense crown. Leaves 10–38cm
long, opposite, oblong-obovate. Flowers 5–7cm across,
reddish-pink, clustered on leafless branches. Fruits 5–8cm
across, ellipsoid, dark red with white or pink streaks.
DISTRIBUTION AND ECOLOGY Presumably originated
in SE Asia. Now cultivated throughout the humid tropics,
especially in SE Asia, S Asia and the Pacific. **USES** Large,
crisp-fleshed fruits, faintly tasting of cloves, are eaten raw
and often used in preserves with other fruits.

Syzygium myrtifolium ■ Red Lip (*Kelat Paya*)

DESCRIPTION Medium-sized evergreen tree to 20m
tall. Leaves *c*. 7.5cm long, elliptic to lanceolate,
opposite, young leaves distinctively reddish, turning
brown, then green. Flowers *c*. 2cm across, in terminal
and subterminal axillary clusters, white. Fruits *c*. 9mm
across, globose or ellipsoid, ripening dark purple to
black. **DISTRIBUTION AND ECOLOGY** NE India,
Myanmar, Thailand, Sumatra, Peninsular Malaysia,
Borneo and the Philippines. Evergreen forests to 1,000m
altitude. **USES** In recent decades this species has become
popular in cultivation as a tree; it can also be easily
pruned to any shape. The new leaf flush is an attractive
red, and there is a variety with a maroon flush.

Syzygium zeylanicum ■ Spicate Eugenia
(*Kelat Nasi, Gelam Tikus*)

DESCRIPTION Small evergreen bushy tree to 15m tall. Bark becomes orange-brown, and thinly papery flaky. Leaves 2.5–8cm long, lanceolate to elliptic, opposite. Flowers 2.4–4cm long, white, in terminal or axillary clusters. Fruits *c.* 6mm across, globose, ripening white. **DISTRIBUTION AND ECOLOGY** Madagascar, China, India, Sri Lanka, Bangladesh, Myanmar, Thailand, Malaysia and Indonesia. Common on degraded land and in old secondary forests, over sand near coasts, on rocky hilltops to hill forests, to 1,300m altitude. **USES** Sometimes planted as an ornamental. When fruiting, attractive white fruits cover whole crown.

Xanthostemon chrysanthus
■ Golden Penda (Golden Myrtle)

DESCRIPTION Medium-sized evergreen tree to 40m
tall. Leaves 8–25cm long, elliptic to lanceolate. Flowers
c. 3cm across, bright yellow, in terminal clusters. Fruits
12–14mm across, globose, capsular. **DISTRIBUTION
AND ECOLOGY** Endemic in NE Queensland. Frequent
on creek banks near sea level to 600m in open forests
and rainforests. **USES** Widely planted as an ornamental
for its attractive flowers. Whole tree blooms yellow
during the flowering season.

OXALIDACEAE (STARFRUITS)

Averrhoa bilimbi
■ Cucumber Tree (*Belimbing, Bilimbi*)

DESCRIPTION Small evergreen tree
5–10m tall. Leaves pinnately compound
with terminal leaflet, 30– 60cm long,
6–20 leaflets on each side of rachis.
Flowers *c.* 1.5cm across, purplish-red,
borne in pendulous cluster on main
trunk and branches. Fruits 4–10cm long,
ellipsoid to obovoid, light green ripening
yellowish-green. **DISTRIBUTION AND
ECOLOGY** Possibly native in Moluccas.
Widely cultivated as a fruit tree.
Naturalized in some countries. **USES**
Fruits edible, eaten raw although very
sour, and sometimes pickled. Often used
as a flavouring in sour dishes.

Averrhoa carambola
■ Starfruit (Carambola, *Belimbing Manis*)

DESCRIPTION Small evergreen tree 3–5m tall. Leaves pinnately compound with terminal leaflets, 15–25cm long, 3–4 leaflets on each side of rachis. Flowers 2–5cm long, light purple, clustered in axils of old leaves on branches. Fruits 5–8cm long, ellipsoid, with characteristic shape in cross-section resembling a 5-pointed star, yellowish-green when ripe. **DISTRIBUTION AND ECOLOGY** Widely cultivated in tropical areas. Unknown in the wild. Probably native in Java and Moluccas. **USES** Fruits edible, and both sweet and sour varieties are available.

PHYLLANTHACEAE (RAMBAI)

Baccaurea lanceolata ■ Green Rambai (*Rambai Utan, Assam Pahong*)

DESCRIPTION Small to medium-sized evergreen tree to 30m tall. Leaves 9–45cm long, ovate to obovate. Flowers unisexual, with male and female flowers on separate trees. Male flowers yellow to pink to purple to cream-white, in spikes clustered on trunk and main branches; female flowers yellow to orange to purple, in spikes also clustered on trunk. Fruits 2.5–5cm long, globose to ellipsoid, green to yellow to whitish to grey when ripe. **DISTRIBUTION AND ECOLOGY** Thailand, Peninsular Malaysia, Sumatra, N Java, Borneo and Palawan. Lowland rainforests to 1,300m elevation. **USES** Fruits edible but sour. Rarely in cultivation.

Baccaurea ramiflora
■ Burmese Grape (*Tampoi*)

DESCRIPTION Small evergreen tree to 15m tall.
Leaves 10–22cm long, narrowly elliptic to obovate.
Flowers unisexual, with male and female flowers
on separate trees. Male flowers yellow, in spikes
clustered on trunks and branches; female flowers
bright red, in spikes, also clustered on main trunk
and older branches. Fruits 2.5–3.5cm long, pale
orange ripening red, ovoid to ellipsoid or spherical.
DISTRIBUTION AND ECOLOGY Throughout
Peninsular Malaysia and northwards to Assam
and Yunnan. Lowland evergreen forests to 1,250m
elevation. **USES** Fruits edible but sour-sweet.

Bridelia tomentosa
■ *Kenidia* (*Kernong, Kernam*)

DESCRIPTION Evergreen shrub to small tree to 13m tall, with slender, whip-like branches. Leaves 3–9cm long, elliptic to linear-lanceolate. Flowers unisexual, with male and female flowers on the same tree in clusters at axils of leaves. Fruits 4–7mm across, globose, green, ripening brown-red to black.
DISTRIBUTION AND ECOLOGY S China, Hainan, Taiwan, Nepal, SE Asia to N Australia. In secondary vegetation and forest edges of deciduous to evergreen forests.

Phyllanthus acidus
■ Malay Gooseberry (Otaheite Gooseberry, *Chermai*)

DESCRIPTION Small deciduous shrub to small tree

5–10m tall. Leaves 2–7.5cm long, simple, distichous, elliptic to oblong-elliptic. Flowers unisexual and bisexual, with male and female flowers on the same tree, on leafless parts of main branches, pinkish. Fruits *c.* 2cm across, globular with longitudinal ribs, densely clustered, pale yellow to white. **DISTRIBUTION AND ECOLOGY** Only known in cultivation; origin unknown. Widely cultivated in the tropics. **USES** Fruits edible but very sour, and often pickled.

Phyllanthus emblica
■ Malacca Tree (Indian Gooseberry, Emblic)

DESCRIPTION Small deciduous tree to
23m tall. Leaves simple, 8–23mm long,
distichous. Flowers unisexual, with male
and female flowers on the same tree, in
axils of leaves, yellow. Fruits 1–1.3cm
across, globose with fleshy exocarp,
pale green ripening yellowish-white.
DISTRIBUTION AND ECOLOGY S
China, Taiwan, Bhutan, Nepal, India, Sri
Lanka, Myanmar, Thailand, Cambodia,
Laos, Peninsular Malaysia and Indonesia.
Open areas of deciduous and evergreen
forests. **USES** Fruits edible but very sour,
and often pickled with sugar.

RUBIACEAE (COFFEE)

Coffea canephora ■ Robusta Coffee

DESCRIPTION Evergreen shrub or small tree to 12m tall. Leaves 15–30cm long, oppositely arranged, elliptic, elliptic-oblong. Flowers *c.* 4cm across, clustered at axils of leaves, tubular, white to pink. Fruits 10–12mm across, subglobose, ripening red. **DISTRIBUTION AND ECOLOGY**

Widely cultivated in SE Asia, particularly in Vietnam and Indonesia as lowland coffee. Upland forests of Ethiopia, W and C Africa. **USES** Seeds roasted to produce coffee beans. Higher yields and easier to grow than *C. arabica*, the mountain coffee.

Gardenia carinata
■ Kedah Gardenia (*Mentiong Kedah*)

DESCRIPTION Small evergreen tree to 15m tall. Leaves 7–25cm long, oppositely arranged, obovate. Flowers 5–8cm

across, solitary or in clusters of a few, tubular, cream to yellow turning orange. Fruits *c.* 2.5cm across, ribbed, ellipsoid to globose indehiscent. **DISTRIBUTION AND ECOLOGY** Thailand and Peninsular Malaysia. Lowland evergreen forests. **USES** Often planted as an ornamental.

Gardenia tubifera
■ Water Gardenia (*Mentiong Bukit*)

DESCRIPTION
Small to medium-
sized evergreen
tree often 8–15m
tall, reaching 25m.
Leaves 5–26cm long,
oppositely arranged,
obovate. Flowers
solitary, 3–9cm
across, tubular,
white to pale yellow,
turning orange. Fruits

1.5–5cm across, globose, smooth, splitting into 5–8 parts, exposing seeds in an orange to reddish pulp. **DISTRIBUTION AND ECOLOGY** Thailand, Peninsular Malaysia, Sumatra and Borneo. Lowland to hill evergreen forests. **USES** Occasionally planted as an ornamental.

Greenea corymbosa
■ Tinjau Belukar (*Ulai Ulai*)

DESCRIPTION Shrub to small evergreen tree
c. 10m tall. Leaves 20–35cm long, oppositely
arranged, oblanceolate. Flowers 5–7mm long in
terminal clusters, tubular, white turning pink.
Fruits 2–3.5cm across, a capsule, splitting into
2 when ripe. **DISTRIBUTION AND ECOLOGY**
Myanmar, Thailand and Peninsular Malaysia.
Rocky coasts to hill ridges. Frequent in secondary
forests and near streams.

Guettarda speciosa ■ Beach Gardenia
(Sea Randia, Zebra Wood, *Selar Makan*)

DESCRIPTION Evergreen shrub to small tree to 10m tall, frequently multi-trunked. Leaves 9–24cm long, broadly obovate, oppositely arranged. Flowers 17–35mm long, tubular, white, velvety short-hairy in axillary clusters. Fruits 1.5–2.5cm across, depressed globose. **DISTRIBUTION AND ECOLOGY** Africa to SE Asia and Pacific islands. Common tree of seashores.

Ixora congesta
■ Malayan Ixora

DESCRIPTION Evergreen shrub to treelet to 6m tall. Leaves 12–30cm long, elliptic to oblong, oppositely arranged. Flowers in many-flowered terminal clusters, 15–20cm across, tubular, yellow turning reddish-orange, not scented. Fruits 7–12mm across, globose ripening red to purplish-black. **DISTRIBUTION AND ECOLOGY** S Myanmar, Peninsular Malaysia to Moluccan Islands. Evergreen lowland rainforests. **USES** Often cultivated as an ornamental shrub.

Ixora finlaysoniana ■ Siamese White Ixora

DESCRIPTION Evergreen shrub 5–6m tall. Leaves
10–17cm long, elliptic-oblong to elliptic, to obovate,
oppositely arranged. Flowers in many-flowered
terminal clusters to 8cm
wide, tubular, white,
fragrant. Fruits *c.* 0.8cm
across, subglobose,
ripening reddish-black.
**DISTRIBUTION AND
ECOLOGY** India, Indo-
China, Thailand and the
Philippines. Evergreen
lowland forests. **USES**
Often cultivated as an
ornamental shrub.

Morinda citrifolia ■ Noni (Indian Mulberry, Cheese Fruit, *Mengkudu Duan Besar*)

DESCRIPTION Small evergreen tree to *c.* 9m tall.
Leaves *c.* 30cm long, oppositely arranged, broadly
elliptic to obovate. Flowers on solitary heads,
0.8–3cm across, corolla tube 10–12mm long, tubular,
white. Fruiting heads oblong to ovoid, 1.2–5.5cm
long, ripening whitish to yellowish. **DISTRIBUTION
AND ECOLOGY** India to Indo-China and SE Asia.
Lowland forests and rocky coasts. **USES** Often
cultivated in villages for its fruits.

Porterandia anisophylla

■ Wild Randia (*Tinjau Belukar*)

DESCRIPTION Small evergreen tree to 12m tall. Leaves 12–35cm long, obovate, oppositely arranged; opposing leaves of unequal sizes in branches. Flowers 11–13mm long, tubular, white. Fruits 2.5–3.5cm across, globose with persistent calyx apically, smooth. **DISTRIBUTION AND ECOLOGY** Sumatra, Peninsular Malaysia and Borneo, where it is a very common understorey tree. Lowland to mountain evergreen forests.

Rothmannia schoemanii ■ Crow's Mallet Tree (*Kelompang Gajah*)

DESCRIPTION Medium-sized evergreen tree to 30m tall. Crown loose and spreading. Leaves 9–17cm long, oppositely arranged, elliptic to obovate. Flowers 5–7cm long, funnel shaped, white with purple markings and speckles inside. Fruits 3–8cm across, globose, smooth. **DISTRIBUTION AND ECOLOGY** Myanmar, Thailand, Peninsular Malaysia, Sumatra, Java and Borneo. Lowland to hill evergreen forests. **USES** Handsome tree with very attractive flowers, with potential as an ornamental.

RUTACEAE (CITRUSES)

Aegle marmelos ■ Bengal Quince (Maja, *Bael*)

DESCRIPTION Small deciduous tree to 15m tall. Leaves
10–15cm long, trifoliate. Flowers greenish-white, scented,
in axillary clusters. Fruits 5–20cm across, globose, green
or greyish, then yellow. **DISTRIBUTION AND ECOLOGY**
India. Subtropical monsoonal climate. **USES** Fruits edible.
Eaten raw or made into jam and drinks, and used as
traditional medicine. Flowers distilled to make perfumes.

Murraya paniculata
■ Orange Jasmine (Mock Lime, China Box, *Kemuning*)

DESCRIPTION Evergreen shrub to small tree 2.5–
7m tall. Leaves 7–15cm long, pinnately compound
with terminal leaflets, 2–5 leaflets on each side of
rachis, 2–3cm long. Flowers c. 2cm long, white,
in dense terminal clusters, fragrant. Fruits 12mm

long, ellipsoid,
ripening red.
**DISTRIBUTION
AND ECOLOGY**
Widely cultivated;
native in SE
Asia and China.
Limestone hill areas,
and lowland and hill
forests. **USES** Often
planted in gardens
as hedges. Flowers
are fragrant.

SALICACEAE (WILLOWS AND POPLARS)

Flacourtia inermis ■ Batoko Plum (Thornless Rukam, *Rukam Masam*)

DESCRIPTION Small to medium-sized evergreen tree to 15m tall. Leaves 5–20cm long with serrated margins, elliptic-oval, young foliage orange-red. Flowers 3–5mm across, greenish-yellow, without petals, clustered along twigs. Fruits 2–2.5cm across, globose, shiny, ripening red to reddish-purple. **DISTRIBUTION AND ECOLOGY** Native in the Philippines and has naturalized in tropical Asia and Africa. Lowland forests. **USES** Fruits edible and crunchy, but sour and acidic in taste. Often not eaten raw but made into jams, preserves and syrups.

SAPINDACEAE (SOAPBERRIES)

Acer laurinum

DESCRIPTION Evergreen tree to 30m tall. Leaves simple, 6–18cm long, ovate to elliptic. Flowers small, with male and female flowers often on separate trees, *c.* 2–3mm long, pale yellowish, clustered in axils of leaves. Fruits a 2-winged samara, 4–7cm across, red, maturing brown. **DISTRIBUTION AND ECOLOGY** Myanmar, Sumatra, Peninsular Malaysia, Java, Borneo, the Philippines, Sulawesi and Timor. Lower montane forests.

Amesiodendron chinense

DESCRIPTION Medium-sized evergreen tree to 25m tall, with dense, rounded crown. Leaves pinnately compound without terminal leaflets, leaflets 3–6 pairs, leaflets 4–15cm long, lower ones symmetrical, upper ones asymmetrical, ovate to falcate, young leaves flushed pink. Flowers small, 1–2mm long, white to pink, with male and female flowers on separate trees, in terminal branched clusters. Fruits 3–3.5cm across, globular, dark brown, with usually only 1 or 2 lobes developed. **DISTRIBUTION**

AND ECOLOGY S China, Laos, Vietnam, N Sumatra, peninsular Thailand and Peninsular Malaysia. Lowland to hill forests, often on riverbanks, to 670m altitude. **USES** Occasionally planted as an ornamental.

Dimocarpus longan subsp. *longan* ■ Longan

DESCRIPTION Small to medium-sized tree 30–40m tall, with spreading, rounded crown. Leaves 10–20cm long, pinnately compound without terminal leaflets, leaflets 4–5 pairs, oblong-ovate to elliptic. Flowers small, *c.* 6mm long, white, in terminal branched clusters. Fruits subglobular, *c.* 2cm across, pustulate and nearly smooth, brown, seeds covered with translucent arillode.

DISTRIBUTION AND ECOLOGY Continental S and SE Asia; naturalized in N Borneo, Java, the Philippines and New Guinea. Lowland forests. Widely cultivated, especially in Thailand. **USES** Planted commercially and often in gardens for its sweet edible fruits.

Dimocarpus longan subsp. *malesianus* ■ Cat's Eye
(*Mata Kuching*)

DESCRIPTION Similar to subsp. *longan* (see p. 145), but different in having leaflets with midribs that are nearly always sunken above, veins nearly always grooved above. Petals woolly and fur-like, especially inside. Subsp. *longan* has midribs that are not sunken above, often raised, veins slightly raised above. Petals mostly subglabrous, sparsely hairy inside. Fruits generally smaller, 1–2cm across, and have thinner arillode. **DISTRIBUTION AND ECOLOGY** Myanmar, Laos, Cambodia, S Vietnam, Thailand, Sumatra, Peninsular Malaysia, the Philippines, Sulawesi and Moluccas. Lowland forests. **USES** Popular local fruit, and commonly planted as a fruit tree in villages.

Nephelium lappaceum ■ *Rambutan*

DESCRIPTION Medium-sized evergreen tree to 27m tall, with rounded, bushy crown. Leaves pinnately compound without terminal leaflet, leaflets 1–6 pairs, 5–28cm long, ovate to obovate. Flowers small, 1–2.1mm long, petals almost absent, clustered in branched terminal and axillary branches. Fruits *c.* 6cm long, ellipsoid to subglobular, covered with 0.5–2cm long, soft, spiny appendages, red to yellow when ripe, seeds covered with translucent sarcotesta. **DISTRIBUTION AND ECOLOGY** Thailand, Sumatra, Peninsular Malaysia, Borneo, Java and the Philippines. Lowland forests. Widely cultivated for its edible fruits. **USES** Fruits edible. Often planted in fruit orchards and home gardens.

Nephelium ramboutan-ake ■ *Pulasan*

DESCRIPTION Small to medium-sized evergreen tree to
10m tall; wild trees much taller than cultivated ones. Leaves
pinnately compound without terminal leaflets, leaflets 1–7 pairs,
4–20cm long, elliptic. Flowers 1–2.8mm long, without petals,
light green, fragrant, in axillary clusters. Fruits ellipsoid, 4–6.5cm
long, ripening purple-red, coarsely blunt spiny, seeds covered
with translucent sarcotesta. **DISTRIBUTION AND ECOLOGY**
NE India, Myanmar, peninsular Thailand, Peninsular Malaysia,
Sumatra and Borneo. Widely cultivated in villages of SE Asia
as a fruit tree. Lowland forests, along streams and on hill slopes.
USES Fruits edible, tasting like litchies (or lychees).

Pometia pinnata ■ Island Litchi
(Pacific Litchi, *Kasai*)

DESCRIPTION Medium-sized tree to 50m tall,
with spreading crown. Leaves up to 1m long,
without terminal leaflets, leaflets 4–13 pairs,
ovate to elliptic to falcate, margin toothed,
young leaves flushed pink to reddish-brown.
Flowers small, *c.* 2mm long, white or yellow,
in terminal branched clusters. Fruits 1–3cm
across, globular to ovoid, ripening purple,
seeds covered with translucent arillode.
DISTRIBUTION AND ECOLOGY Sri Lanka,
India (Andaman and Nicobar Islands),
Thailand, Indo-China, throughout Malesia and
the Pacific, to Fiji, Samoa and Tonga. Common
in lowland forests, often on riverbanks. **USES**
Fruits edible. Often planted as an ornamental.

SAPOTACEAE (CHICLE, GUTTA-PERCHA AND SAPODILLA)

Manilkara kauki ■ Sawai (*Caqui, Wongi, Sawo Kacik*)

DESCRIPTION Medium-sized evergreen tree to 25m tall, often with gnarled and low-branched bole. Leaves 6.5–12.5cm long, oblong, elliptic to obovate. Flowers 1–2cm long, white, clustered along leaf axils on twigs among leaves. Fruits *c*. 3–4cm long, ellipsoid, with smooth surface, ripening orange-red to red. **DISTRIBUTION AND ECOLOGY** SE Asia and NE Australia. Coastal beach vegetation and monsoon forests. **USES** Planted as an ornamental. Wood hard and durable, and used for carved material. Fruits edible.

Manilkara zapota ■ Chicle
(Sapodilla, *Chiku*)

DESCRIPTION Medium-sized evergreen tree to 30m tall, with dense crown. Leaves clustered at shoot tips, 7.5–11.3cm long, elliptic. Flowers pale green, clustered along axils of leaves. Fruits 5–10cm long, rounded, oval or ellipsoid, brown. **DISTRIBUTION AND ECOLOGY** Cultivated since ancient times, and believed to be native in Yucatan and possibly S Mexico, as well as Belize and NE Guatemala. Widely cultivated in the tropics as a fruit tree. **USES** Fruits edible and sweet. Many prominent cultivars are developed, with varying fruit sizes and flavours.

Mimusops elengi
■ Tanjong Tree (*Bunga Tanjong*)

DESCRIPTION Small to medium-sized evergreen tree to 15m tall. Leaves 4.5–17cm long, ovate, elliptic or oblong-elliptic. Flowers 1.8cm across, clustered in axils of leaves, cream coloured, fragrant. Fruits 2–3cm long, ovoid, ripening orange-red. **DISTRIBUTION AND ECOLOGY** India, Sri Lanka, Myanmar, Indo-China, Thailand and Peninsular Malaysia. Rocky headlands and inland forests. **USES** Widely planted as a street tree, for both the tree's form and its fragrant flowers.

SIMAROUBACEAE (QUASSIAS)

Ailanthus triphysa ■ Tree of Heaven
(White Bean, Fern-top Ash, White Siris)

DESCRIPTION Medium to large evergreen tree to 45m tall. Leaves pinnately compound without terminal leaflets, 45–60cm long, leaflets 5–10 pairs, ovate, oblong, sickle shaped. Flowers white in lax axillary clusters. Fruit a samara, 5–8cm long, reddish-brown, membranous, flat.
DISTRIBUTION AND ECOLOGY India, Sri Lanka, Myanmar, Indo-China, S China, Thailand, Peninsular Malaysia, Java, Borneo, Sulawesi, the Philippines and N Australia. Evergreen and seasonal forests to 600m altitude. **USES** Timber used in matchwood and plywood. In India, the incense resin *halmaddi* is extracted from the trunk of the tree.

Eurycoma longifolia ■ Ali's Umbrella
(*Tongkat Ali*)

DESCRIPTION Small, spindly, unbranched tree 6–15m tall. Leaves to *c*. 100cm long, pinnately compound with terminal leaflets, leaflets 5–10cm long, lanceolate to obovate-lanceolate. Flowers reddish, 4.5–5.5mm across, in axillary loose, branched clusters. Fruits 10–17mm long, ellipsoid, yellow ripening red. **DISTRIBUTION AND ECOLOGY** Lower Myanmar, Thailand,

Indo-China, Peninsular Malaysia, Sumatra, the Philippines and Borneo. Well-drained sandy soils, lowland, heath and submontane forests. **USES** Roots extracted and used in traditional medicine.

ARECACEAE (PALMS)

Actinorhytis calapparia ■ Calappa Palm (Actinorhytis, *Penawar*)

DESCRIPTION Solitary feather-leafed palm growing to *c*. 15m tall, 20cm diameter.

Crownshaft green, with 8–10 arching leaves to crown; fronds 2.1–3m long; leaflets regularly arranged, longest leaflets *c*. 45cm long. Old fronds abscised cleanly from trunk. Inflorescence much branched just below crownshaft, with cream-coloured flowers. Fruits on a massive branch, green, ripening orange to red, ellipsoid, *c*. 6–8cm long. **DISTRIBUTION AND ECOLOGY** Native in lowland rainforests of New Guinea and Solomon Islands. **USES** Often planted in villages in SE Asia. Seeds eaten similarly to those of *Areca catechu* (see p. 152).

Adonidia merrillii ■ Manila Palm
(Christmas Palm)

DESCRIPTION Solitary feather-leafed palm growing to
15m tall, but often no more than 9m tall in cultivation,
with *c.* 30cm diameter. Crownshaft light green with about
12 strongly arching fronds; fronds 1.8–2.4m long, leaflets
regularly arranged. Old fronds abscised cleanly from trunk.
Much-branched inflorescences from beneath crownshaft
bearing smallish white unisexual flowers of both sexes in
the same cluster. Fruits are
in large, grape-like clusters
and mature to a brilliant
scarlet. **DISTRIBUTION AND
ECOLOGY** Native in coastal
forests on limestone hills in
Palawan Island, the Philippines.
USES Widely planted as an
ornamental palm. Flowers and
fruits very freely.

Archontophoenix cunninghamiana ■ Bangalow Palm
(Piccabean Palm)

DESCRIPTION
Solitary, feather-leafed
palm to 30m tall,
30cm diameter. Dark
green, red to purple
crownshaft. Pinnate
leaves regularly
arranged in flat plane,
4–4.5m long with short
petiole. Inflorescence
90–120cm long;
originates beneath
crownshaft and bears mauve flowers. Fruits
globose in large bunches, bright red when
ripe, *c.* 1–1.5cm across. **DISTRIBUTION AND
ECOLOGY** Endemic in CE Australia, where it
grows in rainforest or other moist forest from
sea level to 1,000m altitude. **USES** Cultivated
widely as an ornamental palm, although not
very common.

Areca catechu ■ Betel Nut

DESCRIPTION Solitary feather-leafed palm growing to *c.* 15m tall, 20–30cm diameter. Crownshaft green, with 6–8 arching leaves to crown; fronds 2.4m long, leaflets regularly arranged, longest leaflets *c.* 60cm long. Old fronds abscised cleanly from trunk. Inflorescence much branched just below crownshaft, with cream-coloured flowers. Fruits on a massive branch, green, ripening yellow to red, ellipsoid, *c.* 4–5cm long. **DISTRIBUTION AND ECOLOGY** Origin unknown; probably native in the Philippines. **USES** Widely planted for its nuts. Betel nuts are mildly narcotic and locals chew them mixed with leaves of the Pepper Vine Piper betle, slaked lime, and sometimes additional herbs and spices, to obtain the narcotic effect.

Arenga obtusifolia ■ *Kerjim*

DESCRIPTION Loosely clustering, feather-leafed palm growing to 15m tall, *c.* 50cm diameter. Leaf sheath only persistent for short distance underneath crown, subsequently abscising cleanly and leaving a clean trunk with clear, ladder-like nodes. Fronds slightly smaller than those of both A. *pinnata* and A. *westerhoutii* (see opposite), leaflets regularly arranged but displayed in multiple planes. Stems grow continuously, with flowering towards the apex, without dying after the flower cycle (pleonanthic). Bunched inflorescence *c.* 1m long. Fruits ovoid, longer than wide, *c.* 4.5cm long. **DISTRIBUTION AND ECOLOGY** Peninsular Thailand, Peninsular Malaysia, Sumatra and Java. Lowland forests, sometimes growing sympatrically with A. *westerhoutii*. **USES** Inflorescence can be tapped for palm sugar; fruits poisonous but immature endosperms are edible.

Arenga pinnata ■ Sugar Palm (*Enau, Kabong*)

DESCRIPTION Solitary feather-leafed palm growing to 15m tall, *c.* 60cm diameter. Trunk covered with persistent leaf bases with adherent black fibres. Fronds *c.* 9m long and petioles 1.8m long; stiff and erect. Leaflets irregularly spaced and grouped into twos to fours, growing at different angles from rachis, giving a frond a feather-duster effect; linear and slightly jagged at apices, but smooth on their margins. At maturity, stem starts flowering at axils of trunk from apex downwards in an extended flowering and fruiting event, and eventually dies (hapaxanthic). Bunched inflorescences over 2m long, bearing purplish flowers. Fruits subglobose, wider than long, greenish-yellow, 5–8cm long. **DISTRIBUTION AND ECOLOGY** Origin not clearly known, but probably from rainforests of W Indonesia.
USES Long history of cultivation, with young inflorescence being tapped for palm sugar, syrup and alcoholic beverages. Fruits poisonous, but immature endosperms are eaten in desserts.

Arenga westerhoutii
■ Sugar Palm (*Langkap*)

DESCRIPTION Very similar habit to that of *A. pinnata* (see above) – the main differences between the two, among others, are in the leaflet arrangements and fruits. Leaflets of *A. westerhoutii* arranged about evenly along rachis and on a single plane; fruits are rounded. **DISTRIBUTION AND ECOLOGY** NE India, Myanmar, Thailand, Peninsular Malaysia, Cambodia, Laos and adjacent S China. Predominantly wild on hill slopes of lowland forests and bases of limestone hills. **USES** Source of palm sugar, syrup and alcoholic beverages. Immature endosperms eaten in desserts. In Thailand, the collection of immature endosperms is a small cottage industry.

Bismarckia nobilis
■ Bismarck Palm

DESCRIPTION Solitary fan-leafed palm to 12m tall in cultivation, much taller in the wild, 30–45cm diameter. Blade more than 3m wide on stout petiole 2–3m long; covered with whitish wax and scales, giving it a whitish-blue foliage. There are forms with less wax covering that have a more greenish look. Trees are unisexual, with male and female flowers on different trees, borne on tentacle-like branches. Male inflorescence bears tiny brownish flowers; female inflorescence bears knobbly flowers. Fruits 4cm wide, globular, green ripening grey-brown. **DISTRIBUTION AND ECOLOGY** Endemic in N and W Madagascar in open grassland. **USES** In recent years, widely planted as a landscape palm for its magnificent bluish-white fronds.

Borassodendron machadonis
■ Machodo's Palm (*Changkai*)

DESCRIPTION Solitary fan-leafed palm to 15m tall, *c.* 30cm diameter. Leaf sheath persistent in young palms but shedding off cleanly in older trees, leaving behind leaf scars on nodes. Leaf blades orbicular, *c.* 3m across, with green petioles 4m long with sharp knife edges. Trees unisexual, with male and female flowers on different trees. Male flowers bear long orange inflorescence branches with creamy-yellow flowers. Infructescence bears tight clusters of bluish-green, globular fruits, *c.* 8–9cm across. **DISTRIBUTION AND ECOLOGY** Peninsular Thailand and N Peninsular Malaysia. Often in lowland forests and forests adjacent to bases of limestone hills.

Borassus flabellifer ■ Palmyra Palm
(Lontar, Tar, Sea Coconut)

DESCRIPTION Solitary fan palm to 30m tall, *c*. 90cm diameter. Blade 2.5–3m wide on stout, yellowish-green, 1.8m-long petiole. Species is dioecious (male and female plants grow separately). Heavy, roundish fruits, 15–20cm diameter. Each fruit has 3 seeds. **DISTRIBUTION AND ECOLOGY** Widely cultivated. Native in Indian subcontinent and monsoonal SE Asia. **USES** The most important palm in monsoonal Asia, where all parts of it are used. Leaves were formerly used for writing material. They are now used mainly as thatch, and young inflorescences are tapped for sugar; endosperm is edible. Trunk used as construction and building material.

Carpentaria acuminata ■ Carpentaria Palm

DESCRIPTION Solitary feather-leafed palm to 20m tall, *c*. 20cm diameter. Slender grey-green crownshaft. Pinnate leaves arch strongly, 3–3.6m long with short petiole. Inflorescence originates beneath crownshaft and bears white flowers, 90–120cm long. Fruits globose in large bunches, bright red when ripe, *c*. 1.3cm across. Monotypic species (the genus only contains this species). **DISTRIBUTION AND ECOLOGY** Endemic in Northern Territory, Australia, where it grows along rivers and streams of rainforests at low elevations. **USES** Cultivated widely as an ornamental palm, although not very common.

Caryota mitis
■ Fishtail Palm (*Rabok*, *Tukas*)

DESCRIPTION Clumping palm to 4m tall. Crownshaft elongated, 8–12cm diameter. Bipinnately compound leaves, *c*. 2.5m long, leaflets *c*. 15cm long, narrowly to broadly triangular with fishtail tips. Inflorescence many branched, pendulous, *c*. 30–60cm long. Both male and female flowers produced on same plant, but at different times. Individual trunk dies after flowering and fruits maturing. Fruits globose, maturing to black, *c*. 1.5cm across. **DISTRIBUTION AND ECOLOGY** Andaman and Nicobar Islands, and most of SE Asia. Lowland forests, and common in secondary and disturbed areas. **USES** Sometimes cultivated as an ornamental, but gets rather untidy as old stems die off after fruiting.

Cocos nucifera ■ Coconut

DESCRIPTION Solitary feather-leafed palm to 30m tall. Fronds *c*. 5m long, leaflets regularly arranged. Inflorescences simple branched among leaves; 2 woody bracts enclosing inflorescence in bud. Fruits large, green to yellow, ripening to greyish-brown. **DISTRIBUTION AND ECOLOGY** The origin of the Coconut is a subject of debate – it is likely to be in the Indo-Pacific region. The only species in the *Cocos* genus, it is widely cultivated in the tropics. Its fruits are easily water

dispersed by ocean and sea currents. **USES** Coconut products are a major commodity of trade. Copra from the kernel is a source of vegetable oil; young coconuts are harvested for coconut water and the edible endosperm, and the coconut inflorescence is tapped for palm sugar. All parts of the tree can be used as different products.

Corypha umbraculifera ■ Talipot Palm

DESCRIPTION Solitary fan-leafed palm to 25m tall, 60–90cm diameter. Leaf blades massive, 5–6m wide, supported by equally massive petiole 3m or more in length. Produces the largest inflorescence in the plant kingdom on maturity. Flowering and fruiting occur in a single event, producing an enormous panicle, *c.* 6–8m long, with cream-coloured, plume-like flowering branches. The palm produces thousands of globose yellow-green fruits, 3–4cm diameter. **DISTRIBUTION AND ECOLOGY** Widely cultivated in S India, Sri Lanka and SE Asia. Origin uncertain, but likely to be monsoonal region of S India and Sri Lanka. **USES** Historically the leaves were written upon to create palm-leaf manuscripts in SE Asia. The enormous leaves are used as thatch.

Corypha utan ■ Gebang (*Buri*)

DESCRIPTION Like *C. umbraculifera* (see above), but smaller in all its parts. Has spiralling leaf bases, and much more deeply segmented leaves. Also has a brownish petiole, whereas *C. umbraculifera* has green petioles. **DISTRIBUTION AND ECOLOGY** Wider distribution than that of *C. umbraculifera*: NE India, throughout SE Asia, and to N Australia. Lowland in open grassland, and along rivers and wetlands in monsoonal areas. **USES** Leaves used as thatch and widely utilized in the weaving of fans, baskets and mats.

Cyrtostachys renda ■ Sealing Wax Palm
(Lipstick Palm, *Pinang Rajah*)

DESCRIPTION Close-clustering feather-leafed palm to 18m tall, 5–8cm diameter. Crownshaft brilliant reddish-orange to vivid scarlet, smooth. Leaves 1.2–1.5m long on short petioles; petioles and rachis are same colour as crownshaft. Inflorescence red, growing just beneath crownshaft, sparsely branched with whip-like branches. Fruits *c.* 13mm across, globose, ripening black. **DISTRIBUTION AND ECOLOGY** Native in peat-swamp forests of Thailand, Sumatra, Peninsular Malaysia and Borneo. **USES** Widely planted for its brilliant red crownshaft.

Dictyosperma album
■ Princess Palm

DESCRIPTION Solitary feather-leafed palm to 9m tall, *c.* 15cm diameter, with swollen base. Crownshaft light green to grey, to almost white. Leaves 2.4–3.6m long, leaflets regularly arranged. Inflorescence *c.* 60cm long, just below crownshaft, simply branched and enclosed in 2 bracts in bud stage. Fruits ovoid to ovoid-ellipsoid, *c.* 1.5cm long, ripening black or purplish. **DISTRIBUTION AND ECOLOGY** Endemic in Mascarene Islands. Close to extinction in the wild. **USES** Often planted as an ornamental palm.

Dypsis decaryi
■ Triangular Palm

DESCRIPTION Solitary feather-leafed palm to 10m tall, *c*. 50cm diameter. Crownshaft grey to white, leaf sheaths arranged in 3 overlapping rows or ranks, giving trunk a triangular shape. Young leaves and sheaths covered with rusty-brown tomentum. Leaves 10m long, leaflets stiffy erect, regularly arranged, covered with greyish tomentum. Inflorescence grows within lower leaf sheaths, much branched, 1.2–1.5m long. Fruits *c*. 2.5cm across, ovoid, greenish-yellow to white. **DISTRIBUTION AND ECOLOGY** Endemic in Madagascar's rainforests. **USES** Widely cultivated as an ornamental.

Dypsis leptocheilos ■ Redneck Palm
(Teddy Bear Palm)

DESCRIPTION Solitary feather-leafed palm to 20m tall, 25–38cm diameter. Crownshaft and leaf bases covered with deep orange-brown to reddish-brown, velvety hairs. Leaves 3.6m long, with regularly arranged leaflets. Inflorescence just below crownshaft, much branched, to *c*. 60cm long. Fruits globose *c*. 2cm across, ripening creamy-yellow. **DISTRIBUTION AND ECOLOGY** Endemic in Madagascar. **USES** Widely cultivated as an ornamental.

Dypsis lutescens
■ Yellow Cane Palm (Golden Cane Palm)

DESCRIPTION Close-clustering feather-leafed palm to 8m tall; green, yellow-orange-ringed stem, 5–8cm diameter. Crownshaft greyish-green to almost silvery-grey, slightly bulging at base. Leaves 1.8–2.5m long, beautifully arched, leaflets regularly arranged in V-shaped plane. Inflorescence grows among leaf sheaths, pendent, branched. Fruits ovoid, yellow-orange, *c.* 2.5cm long. **DISTRIBUTION AND ECOLOGY** Endemic in Madagascar. Critically Endangered in the wild. **USES** Ironically, one of the most common palms in cultivation. Very tolerant of both shade and full sun.

Dypsis madagascariensis
■ Butterfly Palm (Malagasy Palm)

DESCRIPTION Solitary, sometime close-clustering, feather-leafed palm to 8m tall, *c.* 15cm diameter. Stem

base sometimes swollen. Crownshaft greyish to white. Leaves to 3m long, leaflets irregularly spaced, arranged in groups in several planes, giving a plumose appearance. Inflorescence grows just below crownshaft, much branched. Fruits ovoid, *c.* 1.6cm long, brown when ripe. **DISTRIBUTION AND ECOLOGY** Endemic in N Madagascar in dry, open areas of semi-deciduous forests. **USES** Widely cultivated as an ornamental.

Elaeis guineensis
■ African Oil Palm

DESCRIPTION
Solitary feather-leafed palm to 18m tall, often shorter in cultivation, *c.* 60cm diameter. Leaves 4.5m long, erect but gently arching near ends, leaflets irregularly arranged in clusters and spread in several planes. Male and

female inflorescences produced on different shoots but on the same palm in between leaves. Fruits produced in dense bunch, up to 5cm long, ovoid, black to red. **DISTRIBUTION AND ECOLOGY** Native in moist tropical W and C Africa. In open forests, often along edges of rivers. **USES** Widely cultivated as an important edible oil-producing palm (from fruits).

Euterpe edulis ■ Assai Palm (Palmito)

DESCRIPTION Mostly solitary, sometimes clustering, feather-leafed palm to 9m tall, *c.* 15cm diameter. Crownshaft olive-green to deep green with suffusion of orange or red. Leaves *c.* 3m long, with stiff rachises and regularly spaced, drooping leaflets. Inflorescences consist of many thin branches, growing beneath crownshaft.

Flowers tiny, whitish. Fruits globose, 13mm across, dark purple to black when mature. **DISTRIBUTION AND ECOLOGY** Native in Atlantic coastal forests of eastern Brazil to SE Paraguay and NE Argentina. **USES** Palm cabbage is edible and often harvested; fruits are also edible, as is the unopened inflorescence.

Latania loddigesii ■ Blue Latan Palm

DESCRIPTION Solitary fan-leafed palm to 11m tall, *c.* 25cm diameter. Petiole 1.2–1.8m long armed with small teeth along lower margins; blade *c.* 1m across, covered with fluffy tomentum. Male and female inflorescences borne on different individuals, to 2m long. Fruits egg or pear shaped, 5–7cm long. **DISTRIBUTION AND ECOLOGY** Endemic in Mascarene Islands, in coastal savannah, where it is endangered. **USES** Widely cultivated as an ornamental.

Livistona australis ■
Australian Fan Palm (Cabbage Tree Palm)

DESCRIPTION Solitary fan-leafed palm to 23m tall, *c.* 30cm diameter. Petiole *c.* 1.8m long with spines along margin; blade 90–120cm across, semi-circular to almost circular, segment tips pendulous. Inflorescence sparsely branched, *c.* 1.2m long, bearing small white blossoms. Fruits globose, *c.* 1.3cm across, ripening black. **DISTRIBUTION AND ECOLOGY** Endemic on east coast of Australia from C Queensland to Victoria, where it grows in hilly as well as swampy forests. **USES** Widely planted as an ornamental.

Livistona chinensis ■ Chinese Fan Palm

DESCRIPTION Solitary fan-leafed palm to 14m tall, *c.* 30cm diameter. Crown roundish, densely packed with 40–60 leaves. Petiole *c.* 1.8m long with spines along margin; blade *c.* 1.8m across, nearly circular, segment tips pendulous. Inflorescence much branched, *c.* 1.5m long, bearing small white blossoms. Fruits globose to ovoid, *c.* 2.5cm across, glossy greenish-blue to pale green when mature. **DISTRIBUTION AND ECOLOGY** Occurs naturally in open woodland on southern Japanese islands, Taiwan, Hainan Island and in China. **USES** Very popular as an ornamental.

Livistona decora ■ Weeping Cabbage Palm (Ribbon Fan Palm)

DESCRIPTION Solitary fan-leafed palm to 15m tall, *c.* 25cm diameter. Crown roundish, densely packed with 40–60 leaves. Petiole *c.* 3m long with spines along margin; blade *c.* 1.8m across, semi-circular to almost circular, deeply divided into narrow segments that are pendulous, creating weeping effect. Inflorescence much branched, *c.* 2.7m long, bearing bright yellow blossoms. Fruits globose, *c.* 1.3cm across, ripening black. **DISTRIBUTION AND ECOLOGY** Endemic on east coast of Australia from E Queensland, where it grows in open woods or along edges of forests and in swampy areas near coast. **USES** Widely planted as an ornamental.

Livistona saribus
■ Swamp Serdang

DESCRIPTION Solitary fan-leafed palm to 40m tall, 15–65cm diameter. Crown roundish, with 15–30 leaves. Petiole 1–2m long with spines along margin; blade 1.5–1.7m across, nearly circular, irregularly segmented in groups with pendulous tips. Inflorescence much branched, to *c*. 2.6m long, bearing small yellow blossoms. Fruits globose to ellipsoid, 10–18mm across, blue to purple when mature. **DISTRIBUTION AND ECOLOGY** Laos, Vietnam, Cambodia, Thailand, Peninsular Malaysia, Indonesia (Batam, Sumatra and Kalimantan) and the Philippines. Occurs in freshwater swamp forests, often gregariously. Endangered by habitat loss. **USES** Rarely seen in cultivation, but has an enormous potential as a landscape plant.

Livistona speciosa ■ Mountain Serdang

DESCRIPTION Solitary fan-leafed palm to 25m tall, 20–30cm diameter. Crown roundish, with 40–50 leaves. Petiole 1.4–1.6m long with spines along margin; blade *c*. 2m across, nearly circular, regularly segmented with stiff tips. Inflorescence much branched, *c*. 1.2–2m long, bearing small, greenish-cream blossoms. Fruits obovate to ovoid, 18–25mm across, greenish-blue to light blue when mature. **DISTRIBUTION AND ECOLOGY** Thailand, Burma and Peninsular Malaysia, often growing gregariously on mountain ridges. Also recorded on coastal islands off Peninsular Malaysia at lower elevations. **USES** Rarely seen in cultivation, but has enormous potential as a landscape plant.

Lodoicea maldivica ■ Double Coconut
(Coco de Mer)

DESCRIPTION Solitary fan-leafed palm to 34m tall, *c.* 50cm diameter. Crown roundish, with *c.* 20 leaves. Petiole 4m long, blade costa palmate, recurving, 7–10m long, 4.5m wide. Dioecious (male and female on separate plants). Female inflorescence up to 1m long; male flowers catkin-like and also to 1m long. Fruits ellipsoid, typically 2 lobed, massive, 40–50cm diameter and weigh 15–50kg: the largest seed in the plant kingdom. Fruits take 6–10 years to mature. Seeds require 2 years to germinate. **DISTRIBUTION AND ECOLOGY** Endemic on the two islands in the Seychelles in lowland forests and moist valleys. **USES** Often cultivated in botanic gardens. Because of its unusually large seeds, it is highly sought after by tourists. The endosperm is edible. The species is endangered due to over-collection of the seeds, the sale of which is currently regulated in the Seychelles.

Metroxylon sagu ■ Sago Palm

DESCRIPTION Clustering feather-leafed palm to *c.* 20m tall, 60cm diameter. Leaf crown shaped like a gigantic shuttlecock before flowering. Leaves large, erect, more than 6m long, longest leaflets 1.5m long. Leaf sheath, petioles and rachis can sometimes be spiny. Stem produces a single massive inflorescence in its lifetime; the terminal inflorescence can be up to 7.6m tall with upwards-thrusting primary branches and secondary branches. Fruits are the size of baseballs, light brown and covered with large, overlapping scales. **DISTRIBUTION AND ECOLOGY** Native in New Guinea in swampy habitats. **USES** Widely planted for the starch in its trunk, and very often naturalized in most of the Asian tropics, frequently in swampy ground.

Oncosperma horridum ■ Bayas

DESCRIPTION Clustering feather-leafed palm to 18m tall, *c.* 30cm diameter; stem covered with long, downwards-pointing black spines. Crown pale green; leaves 3.6–5.4m long, spreading, stiff, barely arching; leaflets regularly arranged. Inflorescence grows below crownshaft, much branched. Fruits globose, ripening black, *c.* 1.7cm diameter. **DISTRIBUTION AND ECOLOGY** Native in inland lowland forests of Peninsular Malaysia, S Thailand, Sumatra, Borneo and the Philippines. **USES** Palm heart is sometimes harvested.

Oncosperma tigillarium ■ Nibong

DESCRIPTION Densely clustering feather-leafed palm to 25m tall, *c.* 12–15cm diameter; stem covered with long, downwards-pointing black spines. Crown pale green to greyish; leaves *c.* 3m long, spreading, gently arching; leaflets regularly arrange, pendent to the rachis, appearing like a curtain. Inflorescence grows below crownshaft, much branched. Fruits globose, ripening black with waxy bloom, *c.* 0.5–0.7cm diameter. **DISTRIBUTION AND ECOLOGY** Indigenous to Thailand, Peninsular Malaysia, Sumatra, Java and Borneo. Found mainly in coastal areas, often landwards of mangrove forests. **USES** Trunks are reportedly resistant to marine worms and are often used as pier pilings.

Pholidocarpus kingianus ■ *Kepau*

DESCRIPTION Large solitary fan-leafed
palm to 30m tall, 25–30cm diameter.
Crown roundish, with 15–30 leaves. Petiole
1–2m long, with striking yellow and green
longitudinal strips and large spines along the
margin; blade 1.5–1.8m across, nearly circular,
irregularly segmented in groups. Inflorescence
much branched, to *c.* 1.2m long bearing small
yellow blossoms. Fruits globose, surface smooth,
c. 4.5–5cm across, green turning brown.
DISTRIBUTION AND ECOLOGY Peninsular
Thailand and Peninsular Malaysia in freshwater
seasonal swamps and along swampy valley
bottoms. **USES** Rarely seen in cultivation but
has an enormous potential as a landscape plant.

Pholidocarpus majadum ■ Kepang Palm

DESCRIPTION Solitary fan-leafed palm to 15m tall, 25–
30cm diameter. Crown roundish, with 25–32 leaves. Petiole
1–2m long, with yellow and green longitudinal strips and
large spines along the margin; blade *c.* 1.6m across, nearly
circular, irregularly segmented in groups. Inflorescence much
branched, to *c.* 1.2m long bearing small yellow blossoms.
Fruits globose, surface cracking and warty, *c.* 8–10cm
across, ripening brown. **DISTRIBUTION AND ECOLOGY**
Endemic to Borneo in freshwater seasonal swamps and
swampy sites of heath (kerangas) forest. **USES** Rarely seen
in cultivation but has potential as a landscape plant.

Ptychosperma macarthurii
■ Macarthur Palm

DESCRIPTION Close-clustering feather-leafed palm to 7.6m tall, 5cm diameter; stem greyish. Crown hemispherical, crownshaft light green to olive-green. Leaves 90–180cm long on 30cm-long petiole, erect and arch slightly; leaflets up to 45cm long, arranged irregularly in one plane, with toothed ends. Inflorescence

grows beneath crownshaft, much branched, erect, *c.* 60cm long bearing cream-coloured flowers. Fruits ovoid, *c.* 13mm across, green, ripening yellow to red. **DISTRIBUTION AND ECOLOGY** Occurs naturally in rainforests and low swamps of S Papua New Guinea and N Australia. **USES** One of the very widely cultivated ornamentals in SE Asia.

Roystonea oleracea ■ Cabbage Palm
(Caribee Royal Palm)

DESCRIPTION Solitary feather-leafed palm to 40m tall, 60cm diameter; trunk light grey, slightly bulging (if at all) above swollen base. Crownshaft deep green, with *c.* 20 leaves, roundish. Leaves 4.5m long with *c.* 20cm petiole; leaflets 60–90cm long, growing at 2 faintly different angles from each side of rachis to create a slightly plumose leaf. Inflorescence much branched below crownshaft, flowers cream. Fruits oblong, *c.*

1.6–2cm long, turning purplish to black as they ripen. **DISTRIBUTION AND ECOLOGY** Occurs naturally in N Venezuela and NE Colombia, where it grows along edges of rainforests and seasonally flooded savannah from sea level to *c.* 1,600m. **USES** Often used as an ornamental; very majestic when planted in a row. Cabbage is edible.

Roystonea regia ■ Royal Palm (Cuban Royal Palm)

DESCRIPTION Solitary feather-leafed palm to 30m tall, 60cm diameter; trunk light grey to white; slightly swollen on upper parts of trunk, with enlarged base. Crownshaft green, with *c.* 15 leaves, roundish. Leaves 3.6m long with *c.* 20cm petiole;

leaflets 60–120cm long, irregularly spaced and held at different angles to rachis. Inflorescence much branched below crownshaft, flowers cream. Fruits dull red to purplish when ripe, broadly ovoid, *c.* 1.2cm long. **DISTRIBUTION AND ECOLOGY** Occurs naturally in Mexico to

Caribbean coasts, Honduras and Cuba. Rainforests, woodland and open savannah, usually in wet habitats. **USES** Widely planted as a street tree. Leaves sometimes used as thatch, and palm cabbage is edible.

Saribus rotundifolius ■ Footstool Palm (Java Palm, *Serdang*)

DESCRIPTION Solitary fan-leafed palm to 30m tall, *c.* 30cm diameter; trunk smooth, pale grey with reddish-brown rings of leaf-base scars near apex. Crown roundish, with 20–50 leaves. Petiole *c.* 1–2m long with spines along margin; blade *c.* 1.5–1.8m across, nearly circular, segments rigid. In older palms, leaves are significantly smaller and do not form complete circles. Inflorescences in 3-pronged branches, much divided, *c.* 2.4m long, bearing small yellow blossoms. Fruits globose to ovoid, *c.* 2.5cm across, bright orange-red when mature. **DISTRIBUTION AND ECOLOGY** The Philippines, E Sabah in Borneo, Sulawesi and Moluccas. Low, mountainous rainforests. **USES** Very popular as an ornamental.

Washingtonia filifera ■ California Fan Palm
(Desert Fan Palm, Petticoat Palm, Cotton Palm)

DESCRIPTION Solitary fan-leafed palm to 18m tall, 90–120cm diameter, with swollen base. Unless trimmed, trunks have a skirt of dead leaves below crown. Crown roundish with *c.* 30 leaves. Petioles armed with curved thorns at margins, *c.* 1.8m long; blade

circular in outline, segments with pendulous tips, conjoined for less than half their lengths and accompanied by threads between each segment. Inflorescences grow from leaf crown and extend beyond it, flowers bisexual, white. Fruits mature to black, globose, *c.* 6mm across. **DISTRIBUTION AND ECOLOGY** Native in California, W Arizona and NE Baja California, USA. Grows naturally along streams and near natural springs. **USES** Grown as an ornamental but not commonly planted.

Washingtonia robusta
■ Mexican Washingtonia (Southern Washingtonia, Mexican Fan Palm, Skyduster Palm, Washington Palm)

DESCRIPTION Like *W. filifera* (see above), but differs from it by being taller, to 27m, with a thinner trunk, fewer hair-like fibres on leaves, and tighter, more compact crown. Petioles of this species are shorter and, in younger individuals, are reddish-brown, especially near base of petiole, and always bear reddish-brown spines, even when young. Inflorescences, flowers and fruits of both species similar. **DISTRIBUTION AND ECOLOGY** Native in southern half of Baja California peninsula, USA, and adjacent mainland in Mexican state of Sonora. Grows near streams and natural springs in deserts. **USES** Grown as an ornamental but not commonly planted.

Wodyetia bifurcata ■ Foxtail Palm

DESCRIPTION Solitary feather-leafed palm to 14m tall, 20–25cm diameter; trunk bottle shaped. Crown has 10 leaves. Crownshaft smooth, green, *c.* 90cm long. Petiole short, rachis 2.4–3m long, with many leaflets growing from different angles around rachis, giving plume-like arrangement. Inflorescence much branched, growing just beneath crownshaft, with yellowish-green flowers of both sexes. Fruits ovoid, 5cm long, ripening orange-red. **DISTRIBUTION AND ECOLOGY** Endemic in Cape York Peninsula of Queensland, Australia, where it grows in monsoonal and rocky scrubland on sandy, granitic soils at elevations to 370m. Monotypic palm, with the *Wodyetia* genus represented by only this species. **USES** Very popular ornamental palm.

USEFUL REFERENCES

Ashton, P. (2014) *On the Forests of Tropical Asia*. Kew Publishing, Royal Botanic Gardens Kew.

Corlett, R. T. (2009) *The Ecology of Tropical East Asia*. Oxford University Press.

Corner, E. J. H. (1988) (3rd ed.) *Wayside Trees of Malaya*. Vols. 1: 1–476 & 2: 477–861. Malayan Nature Society. Plates 1–138, 139–236.

Gardner, S., Sidisunthorn, P. & Chayamarit, K. (2015) *Forest Trees of Southern Thailand*. Vol. 1: 1–749. The Forest Herbarium, Bangkok.

Gardner, S., Sidisunthorn, P. & Chayamarit, K. (2016) *Forest Trees of Southern Thailand*. Vol. 2: 750–1531. The Forest Herbarium, Bangkok.

Gardner, S., Sidisunthorn, P. & Lai, E. M. (2011) *Heritage Trees of Penang*. Areca Books.

Heywood, V. H., Brummit, R. K., Culham, A. & Seberg, O. (2007) *Flowering Plant Families of the World*. Royal Botanic Gardens, Kew.

Hodel, D. R. (ed.) (1998). *The Palms and Cycads of Thailand*. Allen Press.

Kiew, R., Chung, R. C. K, Saw, L. G. & Soepadmo, E. (eds) (2012) *Flora of Peninsular Malaysia*. Series II: Seed Plants. Vol. 3. Malayan Forest Records No. 49.

Kiew, R., Chung, R. C. K, Saw, L. G. & Soepadmo, E. (eds) (2013) *Flora of Peninsular Malaysia*. Series II: Seed Plants. Vol. 4. Malayan Forest Records No. 49.

Kiew, R., Chung, R. C. K, Saw, L. G. & Soepadmo, E. (eds) (2015) *Flora of Peninsular Malaysia*. Series II: Seed Plants. Vol. 5. Malayan Forest Records No. 49.

Kiew, R., Chung, R. C. K, Saw, L. G. & Soepadmo, E. (eds) (2017) *Flora of Peninsular Malaysia*. Series II: Seed Plants. Vol. 6. Malayan Forest Records No. 49.

Kiew, R., Chung, R. C. K, Saw, L. G., Soepadmo, E. & Boyce, P. C. (eds) (2010) *Flora of Peninsular Malaysia*. Series II: Seed Plants. Vol. 1. Malayan Forest Records No. 49.

Kiew, R., Chung, R. C. K, Saw, L. G., Soepadmo, E. & Boyce, P. C. (eds) (2011) *Flora of Peninsular Malaysia*. Series II: Seed Plants. Vol. 2. Malayan Forest Records No. 49.

Ng, F. S. P. (ed.) (1978) *Tree Flora of Malaya*. Vol. 3. Longman Malaysia Sdn. Berhad.

Ng, F. S. P. (ed.) (1989) *Tree Flora of Malaya*. Vol. 4. Longman Malaysia Sdn. Berhad.

Ng, F. S. P. (2006). *Tropical Horticulture and Gardening*. Clearwater Publications.

PROSEA 2, 1991. *Plant Resources of South-East Asia*. Vol. 2. Edible fruits and nuts. ed. by E. W. M. Verheij & R. E. Coronel. Wageningen, PUDOC/PROSEA (Bogor, PROSEA, 1992).

PROSEA 5 (1), 1993. *Plant Resources of South-East Asia*. Vol. 5 (1) Timber trees: major commercial timbers. ed. by I. Soerianegara & R. H. M. J. Lemmens. Wageningen, PUDOC/PROSEA (Bogor, PROSEA, 1994).

PROSEA 5 (2), 1995. *Plant Resources of South-East Asia*. Vol. 5 (2) Timber trees: minor commercial timbers. ed. by R. H. M. J. Lemmens, I. Soerianegara & W. C. Wong. Leiden/Wageningen, Backhuys/PROSEA (Bogor, PROSEA, 1995).

PROSEA 5 (3), 1998. *Plant Resources of South-East Asia*. Vol. 5 (2). Timber trees: minor commercial timbers. ed. by M. S. M. Sosef, L. T. Hong & S. Prawirohatmodjo. Leiden/Wageningen, Backhuys/PROSEA (Bogor, PROSEA, 1998).

Riffle, R. L., Craft, P. & Zona, S. (2012) (2nd ed.) *The Encyclopedia of Cultivated Palms*. Timber Press, Portland, London.

Saw, L. G. & Chung, R. C. K. (2007) Towards the Flora of Malaysia, in L. S. L. Chua, L. G. Kirton & L. G. Saw (eds). *Status of Biological Diversity in Malaysia and Threat Assessment of Plant Species in Malaysia: Proceedings of the Seminar and Workshop*. Forest Research Institute Malaysia, Kepong, Malaysia.

pp. 203–219.

Soepadmo, E. & Saw, L. G. (eds) (2000) *Tree Flora of Sabah and Sarawak*. Vol. 3. Forest Research Institute Malaysia.

Soepadmo, E., Saw, L. G. & Chung, R. C. K. (eds) (2002) *Tree Flora of Sabah and Sarawak*. Vol. 4. Forest Research Institute Malaysia.

Soepadmo, E., Saw, L. G. & Chung, R. C. K. (eds) (2004) *Tree Flora of Sabah and Sarawak*. Vol. 5. Forest Research Institute Malaysia.

Soepadmo, E., L. G. Saw, & Chung, R. C. K. (eds) (2007) *Tree Flora of Sabah and Sarawak*. Vol. 6. Forest Research Institute Malaysia.

Soepadmo, E., Saw, L. G., Chung, R. C. K. & Kiew, R. (eds) (2011) *Tree Flora of Sabah and Sarawak*. Vol. 7. Forest Research Institute Malaysia.

Soepadmo, E., Saw, L. G., Chung, R. C. K. & Kiew, R. (eds) (2014) *Tree Flora of Sabah and Sarawak*. Vol. 8. Forest Research Institute Malaysia.

Soepadmo, E., Wong, K. M. & Saw, L. G. (eds) (1996) *Tree Flora of Sabah and Sarawak*. Vol. 2. Forest Research Institute Malaysia.

Stewart, L. (1994) *A Guide to Palms and Cycads of the World*. Cassell Publishers Ltd.

Whitmore, T. C. (1973) *Palms of Malaya*. Oxford University Press.

Whitmore, T. C. (ed.) (1972) *Tree Flora of Malaya*. Vol. 1. Longman Malaysia Sdn. Berhad.

Whitmore, T. C. (ed.) (1973) *Tree Flora of Malaya*. Vol. 2. Longman Malaysia Sdn. Berhad.

USEFUL WEBSITES

Flora Malesiana portal http://portal.cybertaxonomy.org/flora-malesiana/node/1
Flora of China efloras.org
NParks Flora and Fauna https://florafaunaweb.nparks.gov.sg
Useful Tropical Plants tropical.theferns.info

ACKNOWLEDGEMENTS

I wish to thank the present and former Chief Ministers of Penang, Rt Hon. Mr Chow Kon Yeow and Rt Hon. Mr Lim Guan Eng respectively, for their tremendous support for my work and the projects in Penang Botanic Gardens. Dr Ruth Kiew and Dr Francis Ng both reviewed the book and provided many good suggestions for its improvement. I am grateful to Mr Ken Scriven, who made the initial contact, and my introduction to John Beaufoy for this publication. Rosemary Wilkinson for her patience in our many rounds of correspondences and tracking the progress of the writing. I wish also to thank the staff of Penang Botanic Gardens who have helped me in looking out for plants in flower or fruit to photograph. This was the most challenging part of producing this book; particularly Sivakumaran Vasu Devan. I also wish to thank Mr Mohd Azwa Shah Ahmad, the director of Penang Botanic Gardens. Finally, my dearest wife Shu Cheow for her boundless support and love.